KEYSTONE Finish Line

Algebra I

Continental

Acknowledgments

Photo Credits: Front cover and title page: *PPG Place, Pittsburgh, Pennsylvania,* www.istockphoto.com/beright

ISBN 978-0-8454-7371-9

Contents

Welcome to Keystone Algebra I

A central purpose of school is to prepare you for college and careers. With that focus in mind, one of the most important skills you can acquire while in school is a strong ability to deal with mathematical situations. This ability goes beyond understanding magnitudes of numbers and performing operations such as subtraction or multiplication. A solid understanding of mathematics also involves a variety of other skills, including these listed below:

- calculating and estimating with numbers in various forms
- understanding and representing real-life situations using mathematical models
- applying and interpreting equations and inequalities to find rates of change and the relationships among variables
- reading, interpreting, and making predictions from data and graphical displays
- using logic and reasoning skills to solve problems
- relating previously learned knowledge to help solve more complex problems

These skills and more are addressed in the Keystone Algebra I Exam, an end-of-course assessment given no later than grade 11. The test is used to measure how well you have mastered goals set within six different areas of algebra. These areas, or categories, are

- Operations with Real Numbers and Expressions
- Linear Equations
- Linear Inequalities
- Functions
- Coordinate Geometry
- Data Analysis

Within each category is a set of subtopics known as assessment anchors. The purpose of the anchors is to help clarify what essential mathematics skills you should learn in the Algebra I course so that you will be ready to do the work expected of you in college or a career. The anchors are further broken down into standards specifying eligible content; they provide a guide to help your teachers prepare you for the Keystone Algebra I Exam. This book, *Keystone Finish Line Algebra I,* is also intended to help prepare you for the exam by reviewing the anchor topics you have already studied in class.

This book is divided into two modules and seven units, which parallel the breakdown of the assessment anchors. Each unit covers all the anchors within that area of algebra. Within each unit are three to five lessons, each of which reviews the main concepts and skills related to that anchor. Each lesson has the following features:

- the anchor number or numbers addressed

- sections describing each topic of review

- explanations of important concepts

- examples to illustrate the explanations

- sample questions for each topic

- complete explanations for each sample question

- boxed strategy tips, definitions, and formula reminders

- independent multiple-choice practice questions

At the end of each unit is a set of review questions for all the topics covered within that unit. Because the focus of these questions is broader, the review questions are constructed-response, or open-ended, items.

The two question types in this book provide practice with the kinds of questions on the Keystone Algebra I Exam. On the test, multiple-choice items have four possible answers. Each correct answer is worth 1 point.

Each constructed-response item has two to four parts. These parts often utilize skills or concepts that build upon each other. In addition to finding exact answers, you are likely to be asked to show your work, explain an answer, or justify your reasoning when solving some part of a constructed-response problem. Each constructed-response item is designed to take about 10 minutes to complete, and will be scored from 0 to 4 points, based on the level of understanding displayed of the concepts in the item. A brief description of the scoring guidelines is presented on the next page.

- A 4-point response shows a complete understanding of the concepts.

- A 3-point response shows a general understanding of the concepts.

- A 2-point response shows limited understanding of the concepts.

- A 1-point response shows no understanding of the concepts.

Within a constructed-response item, each correct answer or explanation is worth 1 point. So it is possible to receive some points even if your answer is not correct. Note, too, that even if you do write a correct answer, you will not get a perfect score of 4 unless you provide all requested work or explanations. For both of these reasons, it is important that you show all your work or write thorough, clear explanations whenever they are requested in a constructed-response item.

You will be allowed to use a graphing calculator while taking the Keystone Algebra I Exam. Although you may not be required to perform the actions listed below on a graphing calculator, it will be beneficial for you to know how to do so.

- adding, subtracting, multiplying, and dividing, including using the correct order of operations and parentheses

- raising quantities to exponents and finding roots

- plotting coordinate points and graphing them on a scatter plot

- graphing equations, selecting appropriate viewing windows, and using the trace and table functions to locate specific points on the graphs

In addition to having the use of a graphing calculator, you will be given a Formula Sheet for the test. A sample of this is included in the back of this book. While you are not required to memorize the formulas on the reference sheet, it is a good idea to practice using them so you will know how and when to apply them correctly. You can use the sample Formula Sheet as you work through the exercises in this book.

Module 1
Operations and Linear Equations & Inequalities

Unit 1
Operations with Real Numbers and Expressions, Part 1

Comparing Real Numbers

A1.1.1.1.1

Rational and Irrational Numbers

The **real-number system** is made up of rational and irrational numbers. **Rational numbers** can be expressed as the ratio of two numbers, $\frac{a}{b}$, where $b \neq 0$. In decimal form, rational numbers either terminate or repeat. For example, the rational number $\frac{5}{8} = 0.625$ terminates, or ends, while the rational number $\frac{1}{9} = 0.11111\ldots$ repeats.

Irrational numbers cannot be expressed as the ratio of two numbers. As decimals, irrational numbers neither terminate nor repeat. For example, 4.030040005… is irrational since the decimal does not terminate or repeat.

> Rational numbers include whole numbers, integers, and fractions.

> Repeating digits in a decimal can also be written using a bar.
> $0.0363636\ldots = 0.0\overline{36}$

The square root of a perfect square is an integer and therefore a rational number. For example, $\sqrt{4}$ is 2 because $2^2 = 2 \times 2 = 4$. If a number is not a perfect square, its square root is irrational. For example, $\sqrt{5}$ is approximately equal to 2.23606….

Try this sample question.

S-1 Which set includes both rational and irrational numbers?

A $\left\{ \frac{4}{5}, \frac{3}{8}, \frac{11}{12} \right\}$

B $\{-1, -14, 7\}$

C $\{0.\overline{6}, 0.25, 0.1212\ldots\}$

D $\{\sqrt{5}, \sqrt{6}, \sqrt{9}\}$

Choice A shows three fractions; all fractions are rational. Choice B shows three integers; all integers are rational. Choice C shows repeating and terminating decimals, both of which are rational. Choice D shows square roots; $\sqrt{9}$ is 3, a rational number, but $\sqrt{5} \approx 2.23606\ldots$ and $\sqrt{6} \approx 2.44948\ldots$, both non-terminating, non-repeating decimals and therefore irrational. Choice D is correct.

To locate an irrational number on a number line, first interpret the intervals represented by the tick marks between labeled numbers on the number line. Then decide which marks the number must fall between. For example, on the number line below, the distance between each tick mark represents $\frac{1}{4}$ of a unit.

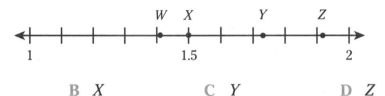

The irrational number $\sqrt{7}$ is a little more than halfway between $\sqrt{4}$ and $\sqrt{9}$. So, the value of $\sqrt{7}$ is somewhere between $2\frac{1}{2}$ and $2\frac{3}{4}$.

Try this sample question.

S-2 Which letter on the number line below shows the approximate location of $\sqrt{3}$?

$$W \quad X \qquad\qquad Y \qquad\quad Z$$

$$1 \qquad\qquad\qquad 1.5 \qquad\qquad\qquad 2$$

A W   B X   C Y   D Z

$\sqrt{3}$ is between the roots of two perfect squares, $\sqrt{1} = 1$ and $\sqrt{4} = 2$. $\sqrt{3}$ is about three-fourths of the way between $\sqrt{1}$ and $\sqrt{4}$, so $\sqrt{3}$ is about three-fourths of the way between 1 and 2. Points W and X are less than or equal to the halfway point between 1 and 2. Point Z is very close to 2. Point Y is about three-fourths of the way between 1 and 2. Choice C is correct.

Comparing and Ordering Real Numbers

A set of real numbers can be compared and ordered easily when each number is written in decimal form. For ease in comparing irrational numbers, they can be rounded to the thousandths place.

For example, compare $-1\frac{3}{5}$ and $-\sqrt{2}$. As a decimal, $-1\frac{3}{5} = -1.6$. As a decimal, $-\sqrt{2} \approx -1.414$. Comparing -1.6 and -1.414 shows that $-1.6 < -1.414$, so $-1\frac{3}{5} < -\sqrt{2}$.

> The larger the digit in a negative number, the smaller its value.

Try this sample question.

S-3 Look at the numbers below.

$$\sqrt{21} \qquad \frac{15}{4} \qquad 4.\overline{3}$$

Which list shows these numbers in order from **least** to **greatest**?

A $4.\overline{3}, \sqrt{21}, \frac{15}{4}$

C $4.\overline{3}, \frac{15}{4}, \sqrt{21}$

B $\sqrt{21}, \frac{15}{4}, 4.\overline{3}$

D $\frac{15}{4}, 4.\overline{3}, \sqrt{21}$

Write each value, or its approximate value, in decimal form.

$\sqrt{16} < \sqrt{21} < \sqrt{25}$. Since 21 is a little more than halfway between 16 and 25, $\sqrt{21} \approx 4.6$.

$\frac{15}{4} = 3.75$

$4.\overline{3} = 4.333...$

Comparing the decimal values shows $\frac{15}{4} < 4.\overline{3} < \sqrt{21}$. Choice D is correct.

IT'S YOUR TURN

Read each problem. Circle the letter of the best answer.

1. Michael calculated the distance between two points on a grid map as $\sqrt{300}$ kilometers. Which point on the number line below is **closest** to $\sqrt{300}$?

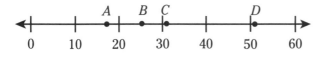

A A

B B

C C

D D

2. Which of these numbers lies between 4 and 4.5 on a number line?

A $\sqrt{13}$

B $\sqrt{17}$

C $\sqrt{22}$

D $\sqrt{28}$

3. Which statement is true?

A $\pi = \frac{22}{7}$

B $\pi < 3.14$

C $\sqrt{12} < 3.5$

D $\sqrt{12} > 3.5$

4. On Saturday, Louise ran $\frac{19}{4}$ miles, Beth ran $\frac{45}{10}$ miles, and Staci ran $4\frac{3}{5}$ miles. Which list shows these distances in order from **greatest** to **least**?

A $\frac{19}{4}$ miles, $4\frac{3}{5}$ miles, $\frac{45}{10}$ miles

B $4\frac{3}{5}$ miles, $\frac{45}{10}$ miles, $\frac{19}{4}$ miles

C $\frac{45}{10}$ miles, $\frac{19}{4}$ miles, $4\frac{3}{5}$ miles

D $\frac{45}{10}$ miles, $4\frac{3}{5}$ miles, $\frac{19}{4}$ miles

5. Which statement is true?

A $5.0 < \sqrt{27} < 5.2$

B $5.2 < \sqrt{27} < 5.5$

C $5.5 < \sqrt{27} < 5.7$

D $5.7 < \sqrt{27} < 6.0$

Unit 1 Operations with Real Numbers and Expressions, Part 1

Read each problem. Circle the letter of the best answer.

6. The areas of three geometric figures, in square inches, are listed below.

$$3\pi \qquad \sqrt{75} \qquad \frac{11\pi}{5}$$

Seth plotted these areas on a number line. Which number line shows the correct locations of these areas?

A
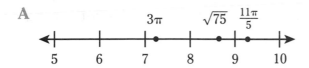

B
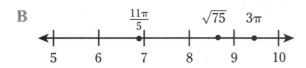

C
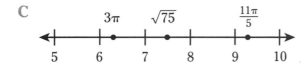

D

7. Which of the following inequalities is true for **all** real values of x?

A $\frac{1}{x^2} > 0$

B $\frac{1}{x^3} > 0$

C $\frac{1}{x^2 + 1} > 0$

D $\frac{1}{x^3 + 1} > 0$

8. Which of the following inequalities is true?

A $\frac{5}{9} > \frac{7}{12}$

B $\sqrt{33} < 4\frac{2}{3}$

C $\frac{13}{3} > \frac{17}{5}$

D $5\sqrt{2} < 2\sqrt{5}$

9. Which inequality is true when □ is replaced with ≥?

A $-5.375 \;\square\; -\frac{11}{2}$

B $-3.\bar{5} \;\square\; -3\frac{1}{2}$

C $\sqrt{10} \;\square\; 4\frac{2}{5}$

D $\sqrt{19} \;\square\; 2\pi$

10. Suppose that x and y are rational numbers such that $x > y$. Which of the following inequalities must be true?

A $x^2 > y^2$

B $-x > -y$

C $\frac{1}{x} > \frac{1}{y}$

D $2x > 2y$

Simplifying Square Roots

A1.1.1.1.2

Square Roots

The **square** of a number is that number multiplied by itself. For example, 4^2, read "4 squared," equals 4×4, or 16. The **square root** of 16 is the number that is squared to get 16, or 4. So, $\sqrt{16} = 4$. **Perfect squares** are numbers whose square roots are integers. For example, 36 is a perfect square because its square root is the integer 6.

Most numbers are not perfect squares. Their square roots can be easily found using the square root function on a calculator or estimated by comparing surrounding square roots of perfect squares.

Simplifying Square Roots

Unless a number is prime, a number or expression under a radical sign can be often be simplified.

To simplify square roots, look for factors of the number that are perfect squares. Take the square root of the perfect square and multiply by the remaining factors. For example, $\sqrt{45} = \sqrt{9 \cdot 5} = \sqrt{9} \cdot \sqrt{5} = 3\sqrt{5}$.

> A **prime number** has only 1 and itself for factors. Note that 1 is *not* prime.

Try these sample questions.

S-1 What is the simplified form of $\sqrt{108}$?

    A $6\sqrt{2}$ **B** $6\sqrt{3}$ **C** $36\sqrt{2}$ **D** $36\sqrt{3}$

> $\sqrt{108}$ simplifies to $\sqrt{36 \cdot 3} = \sqrt{36} \cdot \sqrt{3} = 6\sqrt{3}$. Choice B is correct.

S-2 The expression $2\sqrt{19x}$ simplifies to $6\sqrt{19}$. What must be the value of x?

    A 2   **B** 3   **C** 4   **D** 9

> The original expression is equivalent to $2\sqrt{19 \cdot x} = 2 \cdot \sqrt{19} \cdot \sqrt{x}$. The number 19 is prime and cannot be simplified. Since the 2 before the radical sign changed to 6, you can conclude that 2 was multiplied by 3. Therefore, $\sqrt{x} = 3$. That means $3^2 = x$, and $x = 9$. Choice D is correct.

Read each problem. Circle the letter of the best answer.

1. What is the simplified form of $\sqrt{54}$?

   A $3\sqrt{6}$

   B $6\sqrt{3}$

   C $9\sqrt{3}$

   D $9\sqrt{6}$

2. The diagonal of a computer monitor is $\sqrt{250}$ inches long. Which expression has the same value as $\sqrt{250}$?

   A $5\sqrt{5}$

   B $5\sqrt{10}$

   C $10\sqrt{5}$

   D $25\sqrt{10}$

3. A clothesline is tied from one corner of a room to the other. This distance is $\sqrt{32}$ yards. Which expression shows the simplified form of $\sqrt{32}$?

   A $4\sqrt{2}$

   B $6\sqrt{2}$

   C $8\sqrt{2}$

   D $16\sqrt{2}$

4. For which value of x should the following expression be further simplified?

   $$\sqrt{39x}$$

   A $x = 2$

   B $x = 6$

   C $x = 10$

   D $x = 11$

5. An expression is shown below.

   $$5\sqrt{48a}$$

   If this expression is equivalent to 60, what must be the value of a?

   A 3

   B 4

   C 9

   D 16

6. The diagram shows a window in the shape of a square.

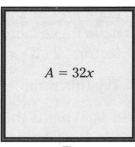

   $A = 32x$

   $8\sqrt{5}$ cm

   Each side of the square measures $8\sqrt{5}$ centimeters, and the area of the square is $32x$ square centimeters. What is the value of x?

   A 5

   B 10

   C 20

   D 40

Greatest Common Factor and Least Common Multiple

A1.1.1.2.1

Greatest Common Factor (GCF)

The **greatest common factor** (GCF) is used when factoring a set of numbers or monomials. The GCF is the greatest factor that evenly divides into a set of numbers or monomials.

For example, to find the GCF of $6x^3$ and $12x^2$, first list all prime factors of each monomial. This includes breaking down variables into prime factors. For a variable raised to a power, n, just like with whole numbers raised to a power, the prime factors are the product of the variable by itself n times.

$$6x^3 = \mathbf{2} \quad \cdot \mathbf{3} \cdot \mathbf{x} \cdot \mathbf{x} \cdot x$$

$$12x^2 = \mathbf{2} \cdot 2 \cdot \mathbf{3} \cdot \mathbf{x} \cdot \mathbf{x}$$

> A **monomial** is an expression of one term that consist of a number, a variable, or the product of a number and one or more variables, such as $-\frac{1}{2}$, x^2, and $5a^2b^3$.

Look for common factors between the two monomials. Both $6x^3$ and $12x^2$ have these factors in common: **2, 3, x,** and **x.** The GCF is the product of these factors: $2 \cdot 3 \cdot x \cdot x$, or $6x^2$.

Try this sample question.

S-1 What is the GCF of the expression $9p^5q + 6p^4q^2 - 15p^2q^4$?

    A $3p^2q$ **B** $6p^2q^2$ **C** $30p^5q^2$ **D** $90p^5q^4$

> Three monomials make up the terms of this expression. Their prime factors are:
>
> $$9p^5q \quad = \quad \mathbf{3} \cdot 3 \quad \cdot \mathbf{p} \cdot \mathbf{p} \cdot p \cdot p \cdot p \cdot \mathbf{q}$$
> $$6p^4q^2 \ = 2 \cdot \mathbf{3} \qquad \cdot \mathbf{p} \cdot \mathbf{p} \cdot p \cdot p \quad \cdot \mathbf{q} \cdot q$$
> $$15p^2q^4 = \quad \mathbf{3} \quad \cdot 5 \cdot \mathbf{p} \cdot \mathbf{p} \qquad \cdot \mathbf{q} \cdot q \cdot q \cdot q$$
>
> The common factors in all three terms are $\mathbf{3} \cdot \mathbf{p} \cdot \mathbf{p} \cdot \mathbf{q}$, or $3p^2q$. Choice A is correct.

Least Common Multiple (LCM)

The **least common multiple** (LCM) is the smallest number or expression that is a common multiple of two or more numbers or algebraic terms. The LCM is used when adding or subtracting fractions with unlike denominators. Before these fractions are combined, they need to be rewritten as equivalent fractions with like denominators. The LCM becomes the like denominator of the equivalent fractions.

For example, one way to find the LCM of 18 and 30 is to list multiples of each number. The first number that appears as a multiple on both lists is the LCM.

Multiples of 18: 18, 36, 54, 72, **90,** 108, …

Multiples of 30: 30, 60, **90,** …

The first multiple that is common to both 18 and 30 is **90.** So, the LCM of 18 and 30 is 90.

Another way to find the LCM is to first list all prime factors of each number. Each prime factor is then multiplied the most times it occurs in either number.

$18 = 2 \cdot 3 \cdot 3$
$30 = 2 \cdot 3 \quad \cdot 5$

The prime factors of 18 and 30 include 2, 3, and 5. The most times the factor 2 occurs in either number is once. The most times the factor 3 occurs is twice, and the most times the factor 5 occurs is once. So, the LCM of 18 and 30 is $2 \cdot 3 \cdot 3 \cdot 5$, or $2 \cdot 3^2 \cdot 5 = 90$.

Try this sample question.

S-2 What is the LCM of $6k$ and $9k^3$?

    A $3k$ **B** $18k$ **C** $18k^3$ **D** $54k^4$

List the prime factors of each term. Then multiply each prime factor the most times it occurs in either term.

$6k = 2 \cdot 3 \quad \cdot k$
$9k^3 = \quad 3 \cdot 3 \cdot k \cdot k \cdot k$

The factor 2 occurs at most once. The factor 3 occurs at most twice. The factor k occurs at most three times. So, the LCM is $2 \cdot 3 \cdot 3 \cdot k \cdot k \cdot k$, or $2 \cdot 3^2 \cdot k^3 = 18k^3$. Choice C is correct.

Read each problem. Circle the letter of the best answer.

1. What is the greatest common factor (GCF) of the monomials a^2b^5 and a^3b^3?

   A a^2b^3

   B a^2b^5

   C a^3b^3

   D a^3b^5

2. The greatest common factor (GCF) of two monomials is $4p$. One of the monomials is $12p^2$. Which of these monomials could be the other?

   A $3p$

   B $8p^2$

   C $16p$

   D $48p^3$

3. What is the least common multiple (LCM) of the monomials $60xy^3$ and $100x^2y$?

   A $20xy$

   B $300x^2y^3$

   C $600x^3y^4$

   D $6,000x^3y^4$

4. What is the least common multiple (LCM) of $25mn^2$, $15mn$, and $10m^2n^2$?

   A $5mn$

   B $5m^2n^2$

   C $150mn$

   D $150m^2n^2$

5. The expression below shows the factored form of the least common multiple (LCM) of two monomials.

   $$2 \cdot 2 \cdot 3 \cdot 3 \cdot x$$

   Which could be the monomials?

   A 12 and $9x$

   B $6x$ and 9

   C $2x$ and $3x$

   D $36x$ and 24

6. A scientist wrote this polynomial to represent the expected speed of a rocket.

   $$12t^3 + 30t^2 + 48t$$

   The scientist needs to factor the polynomial. What is the greatest common factor (GCF) of the terms $12t^3$, $30t^2$, and $48t$?

   A $6t$ C $6t^3$

   B $12t$ D $12t^3$

7. An inventor is designing a machine that will have two gears. The first gear will complete one revolution every $8x^2y$ seconds. The second gear will complete one revolution every $6x^3y^2$ seconds. How often will both of the gears be in their starting positions at the same time?

   A once every $24x^3y^2$ seconds

   B once every $24x^5y^3$ seconds

   C once every $48x^3y^2$ seconds

   D once every $48x^5y^3$ seconds

Exponents, Roots, and Absolute Value

A1.1.1.3.1

Positive Exponents

A number raised to a positive **exponent,** or power, n, is the same as multiplying that number by itself n times. For example, $3^5 = 3 \cdot 3 \cdot 3 \cdot 3 \cdot 3 = 243$. Here, 3 is raised to the 5th power, so 3 is multiplied by itself 5 times.

Try this sample question.

S-1 What is the value of $\left(\frac{3}{4}\right)^4$?

    A 3
    B $\frac{81}{16}$
    C $\frac{1}{4}$
    D $\frac{81}{256}$

$\left(\frac{3}{4}\right)^4$ is the same as multiplying $\frac{3}{4}$ by itself 4 times: $\frac{3}{4} \cdot \frac{3}{4} \cdot \frac{3}{4} \cdot \frac{3}{4} = \frac{81}{256}$. Choice D is correct.

Negative Exponents

Raising a number to a negative exponent models repeated division. For example, $2^{-3} = 1 \div 2 \div 2 \div 2 = \frac{1}{8}$. This can also be written as $2^{-3} = \frac{1}{2^3}$. By moving the exponent to the denominator of the fraction, the exponent changes from negative to positive.

> A positive number a raised to a negative exponent n is not negative. It results in a fraction.
>
> $$a^{-n} = \frac{1}{a^n}$$

Try these sample questions.

S-2 Which expression is equivalent to 5^{-3}?

    A $\frac{1}{5^3}$
    B -5^3
    C $-\frac{1}{5^3}$
    D $-5 \cdot -5 \cdot -5$

5^{-3} can be rewritten as a fraction by moving the base and exponent to the denominator and changing the sign of the exponent from negative to positive. So, 5^{-3} becomes $\frac{1}{5^3}$. Choice A is correct.

S-3 What is the value of $\left(\frac{1}{2}\right)^{-4}$?

    A $\frac{1}{16}$
    B $\frac{1}{8}$
    C -2
    D 16

$\left(\frac{1}{2}\right)^{-4}$ can be rewritten as $\left(\frac{1^{-4}}{2^{-4}}\right)$. This can be rewritten as $\frac{2^4}{1^4}$, or simply 2^4. The value of 2^4 is $2 \cdot 2 \cdot 2 \cdot 2 = 16$. Choice D is correct.

Properties of Exponents

Exponential expressions with the same base but different exponents can be simplified using **properties of exponents.**

- To multiply exponential expressions, add the exponents.

$$(-4)^2 \cdot (-4)^3 = (-4)^{(2 + 3)} = (-4)^{(5)} = -1{,}024$$

- To divide exponential expressions, subtract the exponents.

$$\frac{9^5}{9^2} = 9^{(5 - 2)} = 9^3 = 729$$

- To raise an exponential expression to a power, multiply the exponents.

$$\left(4^{-2}\right)^3 = 4^{(-2 \cdot 3)} = 4^{-6} = \frac{1}{4^6} = \frac{1}{4{,}096}$$

Try these sample questions.

S-4 Simplify $\dfrac{3^2 \cdot 3^3 \cdot 3^4}{3^6}$.

A 3^3 B 3^4 C 3^6 D 3^8

First multiply the terms in the numerator by adding the exponents: $3^2 \cdot 3^3 \cdot 3^4 = 3^{(2 + 3 + 4)} = 3^9$. Then divide by the denominator by subtracting the exponents: $\frac{3^9}{3^6} = 3^{(9 - 6)} = 3^3$. Choice A is correct.

S-5 Find the value of $\left(-2^3\right)^2$.

A −32   B 32   C −64   D 64

Multiply the exponents: $\left(-2^3\right)^2 = -2^{(3 \cdot 2)} = -2^6$. Then evaluate -2^6: $-2 \cdot -2 \cdot -2 \cdot -2 \cdot -2 \cdot -2 = 64$. Choice D is correct.

Powers of Products

A product of powers can also be raised to a power. When this happens, each factor in the product is raised to the power. For example, $(3 \cdot 7^2)^4 = \left(3^{1 \cdot 4} \cdot 7^{2 \cdot 4}\right) = 3^4 \cdot 7^8$.

For any bases $x \neq 0$ and $y \neq 0$, and integer n, $(xy)^n = x^n y^n$.

Try this sample question.

S-6 Which expression is equivalent to $\left(2^5 \cdot 3^5\right)^4$?

A 6^9 B 6^{40} C $2^9 \cdot 3^9$ D $2^{20} \cdot 3^{20}$

Unit 1 Operations with Real Numbers and Expressions, Part 1

The factors, or bases, inside the parentheses are different, so they cannot be combined using the rules for exponents discussed on the previous page. To simplify this, the exponent outside the parentheses multiplies each exponent inside the parentheses: $(2^5 \cdot 3^5)^4 = 2^{5 \cdot 4} \cdot 3^{5 \cdot 4} = 2^{20} \cdot 3^{20}$. Choice D is correct. Notice that even though the exponents inside the parentheses are both 5, the factors cannot be combined by adding the exponents. Only when the *bases* are the same can they be combined this way.

Roots

Recall that the square root of a number is the inverse of squaring the number. Likewise, the **cube root** of a number is the inverse of cubing a number. For a number x, the cube root is written as $\sqrt[3]{x}$. For example, $\sqrt[3]{125} = 5$ since $5^3 = 125$.

Higher roots than square or cubic roots can be taken for numbers as well. In general, for any number x, the nth root of x, written as $\sqrt[n]{x}$, is the number that when raised to the nth power equals x. For example, $\sqrt[5]{32} = \sqrt[5]{2^5} = 2$, since $2^5 = 32$.

> Taking the nth root is the inverse of raising a number to the nth power.
> $$\sqrt[n]{x^n} = x$$

Try this sample question.

S-7 What is the value of $\sqrt[4]{625}$?

    A 5   B 15   C 25   D $156\frac{1}{4}$

$\sqrt[4]{625}$ is the same as $\sqrt[4]{5^4}$. Since 5^4 is 625, the 4th root of 625 is 5. Choice A is correct.

Absolute Value

The magnitude of a number can be measured by its **absolute value,** or its distance from 0 on a number line. The absolute value of a number n is written as $|n|$. For example, $|6| = 6$ and $|-6| = 6$, since both 6 and -6 are 6 units from 0 on a number line.

> The absolute value of a number can *never* be negative.

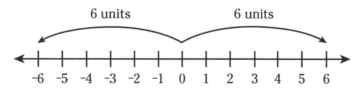

Try this sample question.

S-8 What is the value of $|-8 - 2|$?

    A -10   B -6   C 6   D 10

The value of -8 - 2 is -10. $|-10| = 10$ since -10 is 10 units from 0. Choice D is correct.

Read each problem. Circle the letter of the best answer.

1. What is the value of $(2^3)^{-2}$?

   A −64

   B −12

   C $\frac{1}{64}$

   D 2

2. The expression $3^4 \cdot 3^n$ is equivalent to 3^{20}. What must be the value of n?

   A 4

   B 5

   C 16

   D 24

3. Find the value of this expression.

   $$|-14 + 6 - 12|$$

   A −32

   B −20

   C 20

   D 32

4. Which expression has the same value as $\left(\frac{6^4}{6^2}\right)^3$?

   A 6^2

   B 6^5

   C 6^6

   D 6^{10}

5. Evaluate this expression.

   $$-|2\sqrt{9}| + 2$$

   A −8

   B −4

   C 4

   D 8

6. If $\frac{2^7 \cdot 2^5}{2^p}$ simplifies to 2^3, what must be the value of p?

   A 2

   B 4

   C 6

   D 9

7. Simplify this expression.

   $$2^{-2}\sqrt{48}$$

   A $\sqrt{3}$

   B $4\sqrt{3}$

   C $\frac{\sqrt{3}}{4}$

   D $\frac{2}{\sqrt{48}}$

8. Which expression has a value of 10?

   A $\sqrt[10]{10}$

   B $(\sqrt{10})^2$

   C $(\sqrt{10^4})^4$

   D $(\sqrt[5]{10^5})^5$

Unit 1 Operations with Real Numbers and Expressions, Part 1

Read each problem. Circle the letter of the best answer.

9. The side length of a square is equal to 3^6 millimeters. Which expression is equivalent to the area of this square?

   A 3^{12} mm^2

   B 3^{36} mm^2

   C 9^{12} mm^2

   D 9^{36} mm^2

10. Simplify the expression below.

    $$\frac{(10^{-6})^{-2}}{10^{-4}}$$

    A $\frac{1}{10^3}$

    B $\frac{1}{10^2}$

    C 10^8

    D 10^{16}

11. What is the value of this expression?

    $$\frac{5^0 \cdot 5^4}{5^3 \cdot 5^1}$$

    A 0

    B 1

    C 5

    D 25

12. Which expression has the same value as the one below?

    $$(0.5^3 \cdot 0.2^5)^6$$

    A 0.1^{14}

    B 0.1^{48}

    C $0.5^9 \cdot 0.2^{11}$

    D $0.5^{18} \cdot 0.2^{30}$

Simplifying Expressions

A1.1.1.3.1

A **monomial** consists of a constant, a variable, or a number multiplied by one or more variables, which may have exponents. If the number is 1, it's usually not written. For example, the monomial $1x^2$ is usually written simply as x^2. Monomials are simplified the same ways numeric expressions are.

Multiplying Monomials

To multiply monomials, first multiply any numbers, and then multiply the variables with the same bases. For example, to multiply $(3x^5y^3)(4x^2y)$, remember that $3 \cdot 4 = 12$, $x^5 \cdot x^2 = x^7$, and $y^3 \cdot y = y^4$. So $(3x^5y^3)(4x^2y) = 12x^7y^4$.

> Remember:
> $$x^m \cdot x^n = x^{m+n}$$
> $$\frac{x^m}{x^n} = x^{m-n}$$
> $$x^1 = x \qquad x^0 = 1$$

Try this sample question.

S-1 Multiply $(8ab^2)(5a^4b^3)$.

    A $40a^4b^5$ **B** $40a^5b^5$ **C** $40a^4b^6$ **D** $40a^5b^6$

> First multiply the numbers, and then multiply the variables: $8 \cdot 5 = 40$, $a \cdot a^4 = a^5$, and $b^2 \cdot b^3 = b^5$. Choice B is correct.

Dividing Monomials

To divide monomials, first divide any numbers, and then divide the variables. For example, to divide $\frac{24x^5y^4}{2xy^3}$, remember that $\frac{24}{2} = 12$, $\frac{x^5}{x} = x^4$, and $\frac{y^4}{y^3} = y$. Therefore, $\frac{24x^5y^4}{2xy^3} = 12x^4y$. This procedure applies whether the division is written as a fraction or with a division sign.

> An exponential expression divided by itself equals 1.
> $$\frac{x^5}{x^5} = 1$$
> This lets you "cancel" any expression that appears in *both* the numerator and denominator of a fraction.
> $$\frac{7y^3}{y^3} = 7 \qquad \frac{a^2}{8a^2} = \frac{1}{8}$$

Try this sample question.

S-2 Divide this expression.

$$\frac{30y^2z^6}{5y^5z^2}$$

    A $6y^3z^3$ **C** $\frac{6z^3}{y^3}$

    B $6y^3z^4$ **D** $\frac{6z^4}{y^3}$

Because $\frac{30}{5} = 6$, $\frac{y^2}{y^5} = \frac{1}{y^3}$, and $\frac{z^6}{z^2} = z^4$, the answer has $6z^4$ in the numerator and y^3 in the denominator. Choice D is correct.

Raising a Monomial to a Power

To raise a monomial to a power, raise each part of it to the power. For example, $(3x^4y)^2 = 3^2 \cdot (x^4)^2 \cdot y^2 = 9x^8y^2$.

> **Remember:**
> $(x^m)^n = x^{mn}$
> $\sqrt[n]{x^m} = x^{m \div n}$

Try this sample question.

S-3 Evaluate $(2a^2b^5)^3$.

   A $6a^5b^8$ B $6a^6b^{15}$ C $8a^5b^8$ D $8a^6b^{15}$

Cube each part: $2^3 = 8$, $(a^2)^3 = a^6$, and $(b^5)^3 = b^{15}$. Choice D is correct.

Finding the Root of a Monomial

To take the square root of a monomial, take the square root of the number (if there is one), and divide any exponents by 2. For example, $\sqrt{9x^8} = 3x^4$.

> The square root of x is the number that must be squared to get x. For example, $\sqrt{25} = 5$ because $5^2 = 25$.

Try this sample question.

S-4 Evaluate $\sqrt{16x^6y^{10}}$.

   A $4x^3y^5$ C $8x^3y^5$

   B $4x^4y^8$ D $8x^4y^8$

Find the square root of each part: $\sqrt{16} = 4$, $\sqrt{x^6} = x^3$, and $\sqrt{y^{10}} = y^5$. You can check by squaring the answer and seeing that the result is the expression inside the square root: $(4x^3y^5)^2 = 16x^6y^{10}$. Choice A is correct.

To find the nth root of a monomial, take the nth root of the number (if there is one), and then divide any exponents by n. For example, $\sqrt[3]{64a^{12}b^3} = 4a^4b$, because $\sqrt[3]{64} = 4$, $\sqrt[3]{a^{12}} = a^4$, and $\sqrt[3]{b^3} = b$.

> The nth root of x is the number that must be raised to the nth power to get x. For example, $\sqrt[3]{8} = 2$ because $2^3 = 2 \cdot 2 \cdot 2 = 8$.

Try this sample question.

S-5 Evaluate $\sqrt[4]{x^8y^{20}z^4}$.

   A $x^2y^5z^0$ C $x^4y^{16}z^0$

   B x^2y^5z D $x^4y^{16}z$

Divide each exponent by 4 to find the answer: $x^{8 \div 4} = x^2$, $y^{20 \div 4} = x^5$, $z^{4 \div 4} = z^1$ or z. Choice B is correct.

Read each problem. Circle the letter of the best answer.

1. Evaluate $(10x^4y^3)(3x^2y)$.

   A $30x^6y^3$

   B $30x^6y^4$

   C $30x^8y^3$

   D $30x^8y^4$

2. Simplify:
$$(x^3y^4)^2$$

   A x^5y^4

   B x^6y^8

   C x^6y^{16}

   D x^9y^{16}

3. Simplify this expression.
$$\sqrt{4a^8b^2}$$

   A $2a^4b$

   B $2a^4b^4$

   C $16a^4b$

   D $16a^4b^4$

4. Evaluate:
$$32x^9 \div 8x^3$$

   A $4x^3$

   B $4x^6$

   C $4x^{12}$

   D $4x^{27}$

5. The expression $\frac{24a^5b^3}{6a^nb}$ simplifies to $\frac{4b^2}{a^2}$. What must be the value of n?

   A 3

   B -3

   C 7

   D -7

6. Simplify:
$$\sqrt[3]{27x^{12}}$$

   A $3x^4$

   B $3x^9$

   C $9x^4$

   D $9x^9$

7. The expression $(5a^2b^3)^m$ simplifies to $625a^8b^{12}$. What must be the value of m?

   A 2

   B 4

   C 7

   D 9

8. Solve this expression.
$$\frac{(4m^2n^4)(7m^8n^2)}{m^5n^7}$$

   A $28m^5n$

   B $28m^2n^{-1}$

   C $\frac{28m^2}{n^{-1}}$

   D $\frac{28m^5}{n}$

Unit 1 Operations with Real Numbers and Expressions, Part 1

Read the problem. Write your answer for each part.

1. A surveyor used various methods to calculate the areas of several pieces of land. Their areas in acres are listed below.

$$6\sqrt{3} \qquad (3.5)^2 \qquad \sqrt{75} \qquad 9.8 \qquad \frac{57}{5}$$

   A List these numbers in order from **greatest** to **least.**

   _____ _____ _____ _____ _____

   B Explain how you found the correct order for the numbers in **part A.**

   C The surveyor wrote the related expressions below.

$$6x\sqrt{3} \qquad x(3.5)^2 \qquad x\sqrt{75} \qquad 9.8x \qquad \frac{57x}{5}$$

   Suppose that x is a negative real number. List these expressions in order from **greatest** to **least.**

   _____ _____ _____ _____ _____

   D Explain how you found the correct order for the expressions in **part C.**

Read the problem. Write your answer for each part.

2. Two circular ponds at a botanical garden have the following radii.

   Pond A: $5\sqrt{164}$ meters   Pond B: $\dfrac{25\sqrt{200}}{5}$ meters

   Todd simplifies the radius of pond A this way:

   $$5\sqrt{164}$$

   Step 1: $5(\sqrt{100} + \sqrt{64})$

   Step 2: $5(10 + 8)$

   Step 3: $5(18)$

   Step 4: 90

   One of Todd's steps is incorrect.

   A Rewrite the step so it is correct.

   Answer: _____

   B Using the corrected step from **part A,** simplify the radius of pond A.

   Answer: _____

C Simplify the expression for the radius of pond B.

Answer: _____

D Write an inequality to compare the radii of the ponds, using
the original expressions.

Answer: _____

Read the problem. Write your answer for each part.

3. Three monomials are shown below.

$$12a^2b^6 \qquad 28a^4 \qquad 42ab^3$$

   A What is the greatest common factor (GCF) of these monomials?

   Answer: _____

   B Divide $12a^2b^6$ by the greatest common factor (GCF) you found in **part A.**

   Answer: _____

C What is the least common multiple (LCM) of these monomials?

Answer: _____

D Simplify $(12a^2b^6)^2$.

Answer: _____

Read the problem. Write your answer for each part.

4. An engineer is designing a solar panel in the shape of a rectangle. The length and width are described by monomials, as shown in the diagram.

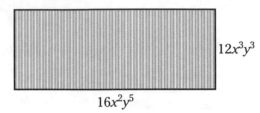

$12x^3y^3$

$16x^2y^5$

A Write an expression in simplest terms for the area of the rectangle.

Answer: _____

B If $x = 2$ and $y = \frac{1}{2}$, what is the area of the rectangle? Show all your work.

Answer: _____

C The solar panel will be divided into small squares. What is the side length of the largest possible square into which the rectangle can be divided? (Assume that $x \geq 1$ and $y \geq 1$.)

Answer: _____

D Explain how you found your answer to **part C.**

Read the problem. Write your answer for each part.

5. The following expressions all use the same values for n, p, and q.

   - $3^2 \cdot 3^n$ simplifies to 3^{20}.

   - $\dfrac{7^n}{7^5}$ simplifies to 7^p.

   - $(4^p \cdot 4^1)^3$ simplifies to 4^q.

   A What is the value of the exponent n?

   Answer: _____

   B What is the value of the exponent p?

   Answer: _____

   C What is the value of the exponent q?

   Answer: _____

   D Explain how you found your answers.

Module 1
Operations and Linear Equations & Inequalities

Unit 2
Operations with Real Numbers and Expressions, Part 2

Estimation

A1.1.1.4.1

Computational Estimation

Some calculations require an exact answer. If you give a cashier $10 for a purchase of $7.26, an exact answer will tell you how much change you should get back. For other calculations, an **estimate,** or approximation, is sufficient. If you want to calculate the distance driven during a road trip, an estimate is appropriate.

For example, a map program shows the distance from Boston, MA, to Sacramento, CA, is 3,014 miles. Andrea plans to drive this distance during a two-week period. She drives 1,327 miles the first week. These numbers can be rounded to estimate the number of miles Andrea has left to drive during the second week.

The number 3,014 rounds to 3,000 and 1,327 rounds to 1,300. Subtract using the rounded numbers: $3,000 - 1,300 = 1,700$. So, Andrea has about 1,700 miles left to drive during the second week.

Rounding is a useful technique when estimating solutions to problems involving addition, subtraction, and multiplication. With division, **compatible numbers** can be used to help estimate quotients. Compatible numbers are numbers that can easily be divided mentally. Some examples of compatible numbers are 500 and 10, 25 and 5, 1,600 and 80, and 81 and 9.

Try these sample questions.

S-1 Tickets to a concert were on sale for three days. The number of tickets sold each day is listed below.

- Day 1: 6,804 tickets
- Day 2: 3,958 tickets
- Day 3: 4,303 tickets

If the average price of a ticket was $19, which number is closest to the total amount of money for ticket sales to this concert?

A $260,000   B $280,000   C $300,000   D $320,000

Round each day's number of tickets to the nearest thousand. Then add.
  6,804 rounds to 7,000; 3,958 rounds to 4,000; 4,303 rounds to 4,000.
  $7,000 + 4,000 + 4,000 = 15,000$

Round the average price of a ticket and multiply by the number of tickets.
  $19 rounds to $20; $20 \times 15,000 = \$300,000$.

Choice C is correct.

S-2 The land area of Hector's hometown is 59 square miles. The population of his town is 35,097 people. Which number is closest to the average number of people per square mile in Hector's hometown?

    A 300   B 400   C 500   D 600

Divide the population by the area to find the approximate number of people per square mile. Use compatible numbers to estimate this result. For the area, 59, a compatible number is 60. A compatible number for 35,097 is 36,000. These numbers are close to the original numbers and they are compatible since they divide together easily: $36{,}000 \div 60 = 600$. Choice D is correct.

Estimation with Fractions and Decimals

To estimate answers involving fractions or decimals, numbers can be rounded before performing the calculations. For example, to estimate the sum of 7.38 and 8.92, the numbers can be rounded to the nearest whole number and then added. So, $7.38 + 8.92 \approx 7 + 9$ or 16. Note, however, that the smaller the place rounded to, the closer the estimate will be to the exact answer.

When rounding fractional numbers, remember to round fractions less than $\frac{1}{2}$ down. Fractions greater than or equal to $\frac{1}{2}$ are rounded up to the next whole number.

Try this sample question.

S-3 Casey bought $5\frac{1}{3}$ yards of fabric for $21.67. Which dollar amount is closest to the approximate cost per yard for the fabric?

    A $4   B $5   C $8   D $12

Division is used to find the cost per yard. Find compatible numbers that are close to the given numbers and that are easy to divide. $5\frac{1}{3}$ is close to 5 and $21.67 is close to $20. The numbers 20 and 5 are compatible: $\$20 \div 5 = \$4$. Choice A is correct.

Estimating with Percents

When estimating the solution to a percent problem, often the percent can be changed to a fraction or decimal before estimating. For example, 28% is a little more than $\frac{1}{4}$ and a little less than 0.3. Knowing this can help you choose compatible numbers.

Try this sample question.

S-4 In a survey of 184 people, 32% like to exercise in the morning. About how many people surveyed like to exercise in the morning?

A 30   B 45   C 60   D 75

32% is close to $\frac{1}{3}$ and 184 is close to 180. Multiply these amounts: $\frac{1}{3} \times 180 = 60$. So about 60 of the 184 people surveyed like to exercise in the morning. Choice C is correct.

IT'S YOUR TURN

Read each problem. Circle the letter of the best answer.

1. Julianna works 32 hours each week. She earns $14.15 an hour. Which is **closest** to the amount of money Julianna will earn if she works for 46 weeks?

   A $16,800

   B $18,000

   C $21,000

   D $22,500

2. Aaron bought a large basket of 59 apples for $22.95. He also bought a small basket of 18 apples for $8.95. Which amount is the **closest** estimate of the cost per apple?

   A $0.20

   B $0.30

   C $0.40

   D $0.50

3. At the start of the year, Mr. Testa's investments totaled $12,352. At the end of the year, his investments totaled $14,118. Which amount shows the approximate change per month in Mr. Testa's investments?

   A $100

   B $150

   C $200

   D $250

4. Rochelle hiked three trails this week. She hiked $4\frac{3}{4}$ miles Monday at a speed of 3.14 miles per hour. On Tuesday she hiked $5\frac{1}{5}$ miles at 2.2 miles per hour. On Wednesday she hiked $11\frac{3}{10}$ miles at 1.95 miles per hour. Which is the **closest** estimate to Rochelle's total time hiking?

   A 9.3 hours

   B 9.7 hours

   C 9.8 hours

   D 10.2 hours

Unit 2 Operations with Real Numbers and Expressions, Part 2

Read each problem. Circle the letter of the best answer.

5. One model of microwave regularly sells for $214. It is on sale for 35% off. The sales tax on it is 6%. Which is the **closest** estimate to the final cost?

   A $130

   B $140

   C $150

   D $160

6. A rectangular tile has the dimensions shown below.

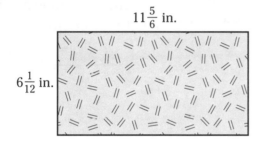

$11\frac{5}{6}$ in.

$6\frac{1}{12}$ in.

   A total of 408 of these tiles was used for the floor of a room. Which is the **closest** estimate to the area of the floor in square feet?

   A 180 square feet

   B 200 square feet

   C 2,200 square feet

   D 2,400 square feet

7. A transit company sold 4,882 10-ride bus passes at $15.75 each. It sold 1,876 31-day bus passes for $47.50 each. Which is the **best** estimate of the total amount of money it took in on these two kinds of passes?

   A $175,000

   B $200,000

   C $225,000

   D $250,000

8. One month, 53% of the dinner entrees sold at a restaurant cost $28 or more. That month, the restaurant sold 2,635 dinner entrees of all prices. What is the **best** estimate of the least total amount the $28-or-more dinner entrees brought in?

   A $39,000

   B $40,500

   C $42,000

   D $45,000

Polynomial Expressions

A1.1.1.5.1

A **polynomial** is an algebraic expression of one or more terms. A **monomial** is a polynomial with only one term, like 8, $8y$, or $8y^2$. A **binomial** is a polynomial with two terms, like $6x - 7$.

> A **term** is a number, a variable, or the product of numbers and variables.

A polynomial is a monomial or the sum or difference of more than one monomial.

Adding and Subtracting Polynomials

To add polynomials, simply combine like terms. See how it works in this example:

$$(x^2 - 9x + 3) + (2x^2 + x - 4) = 3x^2 - 8x - 1$$

To subtract polynomials, change the sign of each term in the second polynomial and then add. For example:

> Subtracting is adding the opposite.
> $$a - b = a + (-b)$$

$$(2x^3 + 4x^2 - 6x) - (4x^3 - 3x^2 + 5x)$$
$$(2x^3 + 4x^2 - 6x) + (-4x^3 + 3x^2 - 5x)$$
$$-2x^3 + 7x^2 - 11x$$

Try these sample questions.

S-1 Simplify $(4x^2 - 6) - (x^2 + 2)$.

    A $3x^2 - 8$ C $5x^2 - 8$

    B $3x^2 - 4$ D $5x^2 - 4$

Changing the signs of each term in the second polynomial gives the addition problem $(4x^2 - 6) + (-x^2 - 2)$, which simplifies to $3x^2 - 8$. Choice A is correct.

S-2 What is the simplified form of the expression below?

$$(6x^2 + 4y^2) + (5x^2 - 3y^2)$$

    A $x^2 + y^2$ C $11x^2 + y^2$

    B $x^2 + 7y^2$ D $11x^2 + 7y^2$

To add these binomials, simply combine like terms: $6x^2 + 5x^2 = 11x^2$ and $4y^2 - 3y^2 = y^2$. So the simplified form is $11x^2 + y^2$. Choice C is correct.

Multiplying Polynomials

To multiply polynomials, multiply each term in the first polynomial by each term in the second polynomial. Then combine like terms if needed, to simplify the resulting polynomial. For example:

$$(4x + 3)(x - 2) = 4x(x - 2) + 3(x - 2)$$
$$= 4x^2 - 8x + 3x - 6$$
$$= 4x^2 - 5x - 6$$

> When multiplying variable terms with like bases, add the exponents.
> $$x^5 \cdot x^2 = x^{5+2} = x^7$$

Try this sample question.

S-3 The length of a rectangle is $5x + 1$ units long. The width of the rectangle is $2x + 5$ units long. What is the area, in square units, of the rectangle?

A $7x^2 + 6$

B $10x^2 + 5$

C $10x^2 + 7x + 5$

D $10x^2 + 27x + 5$

The area of a rectangle is length $\times$ width. So, the area of this rectangle is $(5x + 1)(2x + 5)$. To find the area, multiply each term in $5x + 1$ by each term in $2x + 5$.

$$(5x + 1)(2x + 5) = 5x(2x + 5) + 1(2x + 5)$$
$$= 10x^2 + 25x + 2x + 5$$

Combine like terms. This gives $10x^2 + 27x + 5$. Choice D is correct.

IT'S YOUR TURN

Read each problem. Circle the letter of the best answer.

1. What is the simplified form of the expression below?

$$(2w^3 + 4w^2 + 5) + (3w^3 + w^2 + 4w)$$

A $5w^3 + 5w^2 + 9$

B $5w^3 + 5w^2 + 9w$

C $5w^3 + 5w^2 + 4w + 5$

D $5w^3 + 4w^2 + 5w + 4$

2. What is the simplified form of the difference shown below?

$$(3a^2 - 6a - 1) - (5a^2 - 2a + 3)$$

A $-2a^2 - 4a - 4$

B $-2a^2 - 8a + 2$

C $2a^2 - 4a + 2$

D $2a^2 - 8a - 4$

Read each problem. Circle the letter of the best answer.

3. The perimeter of the triangle shown below is $19z - 7$.

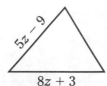

Which expression represents the length of the remaining side?

A $6z - 1$

B $6z - 13$

C $16z - 1$

D $16z - 13$

4. Which expression represents the product of $2xy$ and $3xy + 5y - xy^2$?

A $5xy + 5y - xy^2$

B $6xy + 10y - 2xy^2$

C $5xy^2 + 7xy - 2xy^3$

D $6x^2y^2 + 10xy^2 - 2x^2y^3$

5. A square has a side length equal to $5x - 3y$ inches. What is the area of this square?

A $20x - 12y$ sq in.

B $25x^2 - 9y^2$ sq in.

C $25x^2 - 15xy - 9y^2$ sq in.

D $25x^2 - 30xy + 9y^2$ sq in.

6. A polynomial is shown below.

$$(my^2 - 4y + 3) - (5y^2 + 2y - p)$$

The expression simplifies to $4y^2 - 2y - 4$. What are the values of m and p?

A $m = 9, p = 7$

B $m = -1, p = 1$

C $m = 7, p = 9$

D $m = 9, p = -7$

7. The expression below is a polynomial.

$$wy^2(8y^3 - 2y^2 + 7y)$$

It simplifies to $40y^5 - 10y^4 + 35y^3$. What must be the value of w?

A -8

B -5

C 5

D 8

Read each problem. Circle the letter of the best answer.

8. Look at this expression.

$$(5x + 3)(x^2 - x - 4)$$

Which is an equivalent expression?

A $5x^3 - 3x - 4$

B $5x^3 - 3x - 12$

C $5x^3 - 2x^2 - 23x - 12$

D $5x^3 + 3x^2 - 20x - 12$

9. Which expression represents the perimeter of the rectangle shown below?

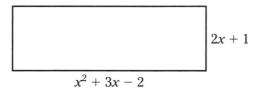
$2x + 1$
$x^2 + 3x - 2$

A $x^2 + x - 3$

B $x^2 + 5x - 1$

C $2x^2 + 2x - 6$

D $2x^2 + 10x - 2$

10. Simplify:

$$(y + 2)(y^2 - 5y + 3) - (3y^3 + 4y^2 - 6y - 10)$$

A $-2y^3 + y^2 - y + 16$

B $-2y^3 + y^2 - 13y - 4$

C $-2y^3 - 7y^2 - y + 16$

D $-2y^3 - 7y^2 - 13y - 4$

11. What values of a, b, and c make this equation true?

$$(2x - 5)(x + 2) + (ax^2 + bx + c) = 6x^2 - 4x - 7$$

A $a = 4, b = -3, c = 3$

B $a = 4, b = 1, c = -4$

C $a = -4, b = -3, c = 3$

D $a = -4, b = 1, c = -4$

Factoring Algebraic Expressions

A1.1.1.5.2

Using GCF to Factor

Recall that the greatest common factor (GCF) is used when factoring a set of numbers or expressions with variables. The GCF is the greatest factor that evenly divides into a set of numbers or terms. In a set of variable terms, the GCF is each variable raised to its smallest exponent. For example, the GFC of m^2n^5 and m^3n is m^2n.

The GCF can also be used when factoring polynomial expressions. The GCF divides each term. The product of that result and the GCF is the fully factored form.

For example, in $ab^2 + ab$, the GCF of each term is ab. When ab divides each term, the result is $\frac{ab^2}{ab} + \frac{ab}{ab} = b + 1$. The factored form, then, is $ab(b + 1)$.

> To check that an expression is factored correctly, multiply the factored form. The result should be the original expression.

Try this sample question.

S-1 What is the factored form of the expression below?

$$40x^4y^3 - 25x^2y^2 - 50x^3y^2$$

A $5x^2y^2(8x^2y - 5 - 10x)$

C $5xy(8x^2y - 25xy - 50x^2y)$

B $5x^2y^2(8x^2y - 5xy - 10x)$

D $5xy(8x^4y^3 - 5x^2y^2 - 10x^3y^2)$

First find the GCF of each term. Start by listing the prime factors of 40, 25, and 50:

$40 = 2 \cdot 2 \cdot 2 \cdot \mathbf{5}$

$25 = \qquad\quad \mathbf{5 \cdot 5}$

$50 = 2 \cdot \qquad \mathbf{5} \cdot 5$ The common factor in all three numbers is 5.

To find the GCF of each variable part, look for the variables with the smallest exponents. In $40x^4y^3 - 25x^2y^2 - 50x^3y^2$, the x variable with the smallest exponent is x^2. The y variable with the smallest exponent is y^2. So the GCF of the expression is $5x^2y^2$.

Divide the GCF into each term:

$$\frac{40x^4y^3}{5x^2y^2} - \frac{25x^2y^2}{5x^2y^2} - \frac{50x^3y^2}{5x^2y^2} = 8x^2y - 5 - 10x$$

The factored form is $5x^2y^2(8x^2y - 5 - 10x)$. Choice A is correct.

Factoring by Grouping

Some algebraic expressions having four or more terms may have a binomial factor in common. They can be factored by **grouping** terms together. For example, consider the expression $6k^2 - 4k + 3k - 2$. This can be factored by grouping the first two terms and the last two terms together:

$$(6k^2 - 4k) + (3k - 2) = 2k(3k - 2) + 1(3k - 2) \quad \text{Factor each grouping.}$$
$$= (2k + 1)(3k - 2) \quad \begin{array}{l}\text{Factor } 3k - 2 \text{ from} \\ \text{each resulting term.}\end{array}$$

Try this sample question.

S-2 What is the factored form of the expression below?

$$12z^3 + 10z^2 - 30z - 25$$

A $(2z^2 + 5)(6z - 5)$ C $(2z - 5)(6z^2 + 5)$

B $(2z^2 - 5)(6z + 5)$ D $(2z + 5)(6z^2 - 5)$

> Group the first two terms and the last two terms together. Then factor each set of terms:
>
> $$(12z^3 + 10z^2) + (-30z - 25) = 2z^2(6z + 5) - 5(6z + 5)$$
>
> Now factor $6z + 5$ from the resulting expression:
>
> $$2z^2(6z + 5) - 5(6z + 5) = (2z^2 - 5)(6z + 5)$$
>
> Choice B is correct.

Difference of Two Squares

Look at what happens when $x + 3$ multiplies $x - 3$.

$$(x + 3)(x - 3) = x^2 - 3x + 3x - 9 = x^2 - 9$$

The result is a **difference of two squares,** since x^2 and 9 are both perfect squares. To factor a polynomial that is the difference of two squares, follow this rule:

- For any real numbers a and b,
  $a^2 - b^2 = (a + b)(a - b)$.

For example, $25h^2 - 4k^2 = (5h + 2k)(5h - 2k)$.

> Polynomials of the form $a^2 + b^2$ cannot be factored the same way as polynomials of the form $a^2 - b^2$.

Try this sample question.

S-3 Which shows the factored form of the expression below?

$$2y^2 - 50$$

A $2(y + 5)(y - 5)$ C $(2y + 5)(2y - 5)$

B $2(y + 25)(y - 25)$ D $(2y + 25)(2y - 25)$

> First factor out the common factor 2. This results in $2(y^2 - 25)$. Next factor the difference of two squares and include the 2 that was factored out first. This results in $2(y + 5)(y - 5)$. Choice A is correct.

Read each problem. Circle the letter of the best answer.

1. Which expression shows the factored form of $a^2b^5 + a^3b^3$?

   A $a^2b^3(b^2 + a)$

   B $a^2b^3(1 + ab^2)$

   C $a^3b^3(b^2 + 1)$

   D $a^2b^5(1 + ab^2)$

2. Which expression is equivalent to $80hj + 64h^2j^2 + 36h^2j$?

   A $4hj(20 + 16hj + 9j)$

   B $4hj(20 + 16hj + 9h)$

   C $8hj(10 + 8hj + 4h)$

   D $8hj(10hj + 8h^2j^2 + 4h)$

3. Which shows the simplified form of the expression below?

   $$90y^4 - 120y - 360y^3 + 30y^2$$

   A $30y(y + 4)(y^2 - 3)$

   B $30y(y + 4)(3y^2 - 1)$

   C $30y(y - 4)(y^2 + 3)$

   D $30y(y - 4)(3y^2 + 1)$

4. Which shows the factored form of the expression below?

   $$100 - p^{16}$$

   A $(10 + p^4)(10 - p^4)$

   B $(100 + p^4)(100 - p^4)$

   C $(10 + p^8)(10 - p^8)$

   D $(10 + p^{16})(10 - p^{16})$

5. A square has an area equal to $4s^2 - 1$ square units. When this expression is factored, which is one of its factors?

   A $(s + 1)$

   B $(2s - 1)$

   C $(s - 1)$

   D $(4s - 1)$

6. Charlotte factored this polynomial by grouping.

   $$3x^2 - 12x + 7x - 28$$

   Which is one of the correct factors?

   A $x + 4$

   B $x - 4$

   C $3x + 4$

   D $3x - 4$

7. The area of a rectangular parking lot is represented by the expression $25x^4 - 9y^4$. The length and width of the rectangular parking lot can be represented by expressions of the form $a + b$ and $a - b$. Which expression represents the length?

   A $25x + 9y$

   B $25x^2 + 9y^2$

   C $5x + 3y$

   D $5x^2 + 3y^2$

Factoring Trinomial Expressions

A1.1.1.5.2

Factoring Trinomials of the Form $x^2 + bx + c$

A **trinomial** is a polynomial with exactly three terms. The general form of a trinomial is $ax^2 + bx + c$, where a, b, and c are real numbers. You can factor trinomials by combining factors of the first and last terms that add to equal the middle term.

Consider the trinomial $x^2 + 6x + 8$. Here, $a = 1$, $b = 6$, and $c = 8$. To factor trinomials where $a = 1$, follow these steps.

Find factors of c that add to equal b. In $x^2 + 6x + 8$, find factors of 8 that add to 6.

Factors	Sum of Factors
1 and 8	$1 + 8 = 9$
2 and 4	$2 + 4 = 6$ ✓

The factors 2 and 4 add to 6.

Then write the factors of the trinomial using parentheses.

$$x^2 + 6x + 8 = (x + 2)(x + 4)$$

Notice that the first factors inside each set of parentheses, x, multiply to equal the first term, x^2. You can check that the entire trinomial is factored correctly by multiplying the two factors together. The result should be the original trinomial. Check:

$$(x + 2)(x + 4) = x^2 + 4x + 2x + 8 = x^2 + 6x + 8$$

Try this sample question.

S-1 Which shows the factored form of $x^2 - 5x - 24$?

A $(x - 3)(x + 8)$ C $(x - 12)(x + 2)$

B $(x + 3)(x - 8)$ D $(x + 12)(x - 2)$

In this trinomial, $a = 1$, $b = -5$, and $c = -24$. Since $a = 1$, find factors of -24 that add to equal -5.

Factors	Sum of Factors	Factors	Sum of Factors
1 and -24	$1 + (-24) = -23$	-1 and 24	$-1 + 24 = 23$
2 and -12	$2 + (-12) = -10$	-2 and 12	$-2 + 12 = 10$
3 and -8	$3 + (-8) = -5$ ✓	-3 and 8	$-3 + 8 = 5$
4 and -6	$4 + (-6) = -2$	-4 and 6	$-4 + 6 = 2$

The factors 3 and -8 multiply to equal -24 and add to equal -5. The factored form, then, of $x^2 - 5x - 24$ is $(x + 3)(x - 8)$. Choice B is correct.

Factors of trinomials can be found using area models shaped like rectangles. The dimensions of the rectangle represent the factors of the trinomial.

Try this sample question.

S-2 The area of the rectangle shown below is $x^2 + 6x + 3x + 18$.

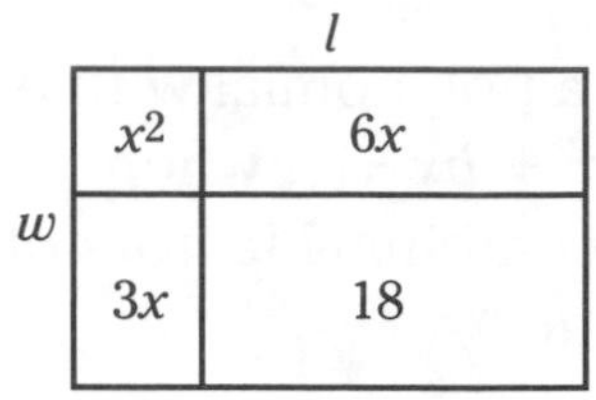

What are the dimensions, l and w, of this rectangle?

A $l = x + 3$ and $w = x + 9$

B $l = x + 6$ and $w = x + 3$

C $l = x + 6$ and $w = x + 18$

D $l = x + 9$ and $w = x + 18$

Combine like terms in the expression for the area:

$$x^2 + 6x + 3x + 18 = x^2 + 9x + 18$$

Then find factors of 18 that add to equal 9.

Factors	Sum of Factors
6 and 3	$6 + 3 = 9$

The factors 6 and 3 multiply to equal 18 and add to equal 9. The factored form of the area of the rectangle, then, is $(x + 6)(x + 3)$. The length is $x + 6$ and the width is $x + 3$. Choice B is correct.

You can check that these dimensions are correct by recreating the area model of the rectangle. Start with the possible dimensions written outside the large rectangle. Then multiply the factors and fill in the corresponding smaller rectangles inside the large rectangle.

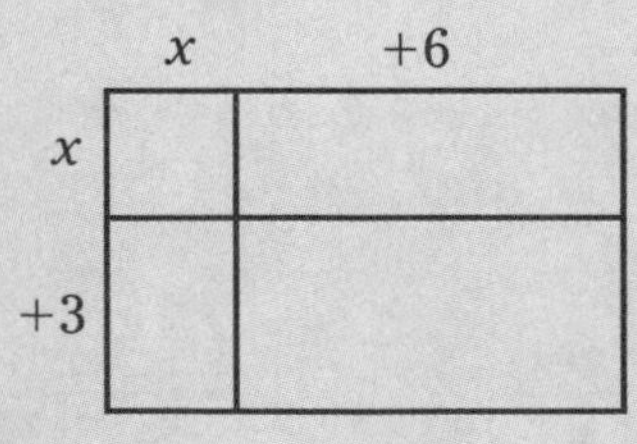

means

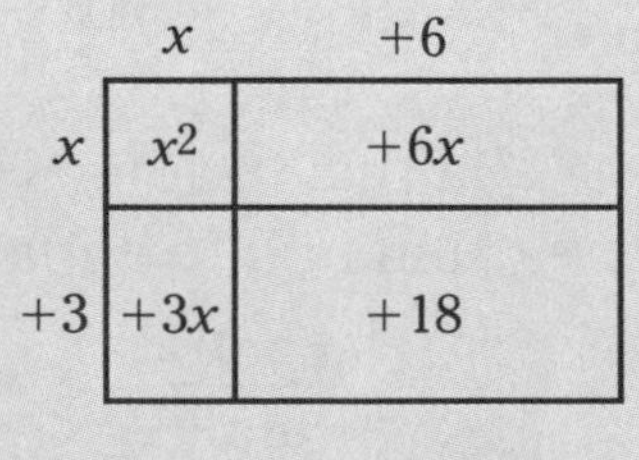

This area inside this rectangle matches the given rectangle, so the factors are correct.

In some polynomial expressions, a trinomial of the form $x^2 + bx + c$ remains after a common monomial is factored out. The trinomial can be factored as usual, and the completely factored form includes the monomial factor.

Try this sample question.

S-3 A polynomial expression is shown below.

$$-3x^3 + 9x^2 + 30x$$

What is the completely factored form of this expression?

A $3x(-x + 5)(x + 2)$

B $3(-x + 2)(x - 5)$

C $3x(x - 5)(x + 2)$

D $-3(-x + 5)(x - 2)$

The expression does not have the form $x^2 + bx + c$. To simplify it, start by looking for the greatest common factor, GCF, of the terms. The GCF of 3, 9, and 30 is 3. The GCF of the variables is x, so the GCF of the terms is $3x$. Factor out the common monomial factor:

$3x(-x^2 + 3x + 10)$

The result is the product of a monomial and a trinomial. Now factor the trinomial in the usual way, into two binomials.

$(-x + 5)(x + 2)$

Check:

$-x^2 - 2x + 5x + 10 = -x^2 + 3x + 10$

So the completely factored form is $3x(-x + 5)(x + 2)$. Choice A is correct.

IT'S YOUR TURN

Read each problem. Circle the letter of the best answer.

1. Which expression represents the factored form of $x^2 - 13x + 36$?

    A $(x - 4)(x - 9)$

    B $(x - 3)(x - 12)$

    C $(x + 9)(x - 4)$

    D $(x + 12)(x - 3)$

2. When the trinomial $x^2 + x - 6$ is factored completely, which is one of its factors?

    A $(x - 1)$

    B $(x - 2)$

    C $(x - 3)$

    D $(x - 6)$

Unit 2 Operations with Real Numbers and Expressions, Part 2

49

Read each problem. Circle the letter of the best answer.

3. What value of b makes the equation below true?

$$x^2 + bx - 35 = (x + 5)(x - 7)$$

A 12

B 2

C -2

D -12

4. The area model below shows the factored form of a trinomial.

x^2	mx
$5x$	40

What value replaces m?

A 5

B 8

C 10

D 200

5. A polynomial expression is shown below.

$$3x^3 - 36x^2 + 60x$$

When the monomial $3x$ is factored out, the remaining expression is a trinomial. What is the factored form of the trinomial?

A $(x - 20)(x - 1)$

B $(x - 10)(x - 2)$

C $(x - 8)(x - 4)$

D $(x - 5)(x - 4)$

6. Which binomial is a factor of $w^2 - w - 20$?

A $(w + 1)$

B $(w - 4)$

C $(w + 5)$

D $(w - 5)$

7. When this expression is factored completely, which binomial is one of the correct factors?

$$2x^2 + 24x + 72$$

A $x + 4$

B $x + 6$

C $x + 9$

D $x + 12$

8. Four expressions are shown below.

1. $x^2 + 2x - 48$
2. $(x + 8)(x - 6)$
3. $(x - 8)(x + 6)$
4. $(x + 12)(x - 4)$

Which of these expressions are equivalent?

A 1 and 2 only

B 1 and 4 only

C 1, 2, and 3 only

D None of the expressions are equivalent.

Unit 2 Operations with Real Numbers and Expressions, Part 2

Simplifying Rational Expressions

A1.1.1.5.3

Simplifying Rational Expressions

A **rational expression** is a fraction containing algebraic expressions in its numerator and denominator. When a rational expression has no common factors other than 1 or -1 in its numerator and denominator, it is in simplified form. To simplify a rational expression, first factor each algebraic expression completely. Then divide both the numerator and denominator by the common factors.

For example, the ratio $\frac{3b^3 + 6b}{18b}$ has $3b$ as a common factor in both its numerator and denominator. Factoring out the common factor results in $\frac{3b(b^2 + 2)}{3b(6)} = \frac{b^2 + 2}{6}$.

Try this sample question.

S-1 What is the simplified form of the expression $\frac{q^2 + q - 12}{q^2 - 16}$?

First factor both expressions in the numerator and denominator:

$$\frac{q^2 + q - 12}{q^2 - 16} = \frac{(q + 4)(q - 3)}{(q + 4)(q - 4)}$$

The common factor in the numerator and denominator is $q + 4$. Because $\frac{q + 4}{q + 4} = 1$, it can be removed, resulting in the simplified expression $\frac{q - 3}{q - 4}$.

Notice that q^2 is *not* a common factor of the ratio. For that reason, it cannot be removed before factoring.

IT'S YOUR TURN

Read each problem. Circle the letter of the best answer.

1. What is the simplified form of the rational expression below?

$$\frac{5x + 10}{10x}$$

   A 5   **C** $\frac{x + 2}{x}$

   B $\frac{5}{x}$ **D** $\frac{x + 2}{2x}$

2. What is the simplified form of the expression below?

$$\frac{6y}{4y^2 + 10y}$$

   A $\frac{1}{2y + 5}$ **C** $\frac{3}{2(2y + 5)}$

   B $\frac{3}{2y + 5}$ **D** $\frac{1}{4y^2 + 4y}$

Read each problem. Circle the letter of the best answer.

3. Simplify:

$$\frac{x^2 - 16}{x^2 + 5x + 4}$$

A $\frac{-4}{5x}$

B $\frac{-16}{5x + 4}$

C $\frac{x - 4}{x + 1}$

D $\frac{x + 4}{x - 1}$

4. A rational expression is shown below.

$$\frac{x^2 - 4x + 4}{3x^2 - x - 10}$$

The expression simplifies to $\frac{x - 2}{3x + 5}$.
What common factor of the numerator
and denominator was removed?

A $2x$

B $(x - 2)$

C $(x - 2)^2$

D $(x + 2)$

5. Simplify:

$$\frac{y^2 - 2y + 1}{3y^3 + 21y^2 - 24y}; \qquad y \neq -8, 0, 1$$

A $\frac{y + 1}{3y(y - 4)}$

B $\frac{y - 1}{3y(y - 4)}$

C $\frac{y + 1}{3y(y + 8)}$

D $\frac{y - 1}{3y(y + 8)}$

6. In the expression below, k is an integer.
The expression can be simplified as
shown. Assume that the denominators
are nonzero.

$$\frac{x^4 + kx^3}{x^3 - 8x^2 + 12x} = \frac{x^2}{x - 2}$$

What is the value of k?

A 8

B 6

C -6

D -8

Read the problem. Write your answer for each part.

1. Jonah and Grace are working on a homework problem together. They are factoring the expression shown below.

$$4x^3 - 12x^2 - 9x + 27$$

A Jonah used factoring by grouping to write the expression as a product of two binomials. What was Jonah's answer? Show your work.

   Answer: _____

B Grace continued Jonah's work, factoring the expression completely. What was Grace's answer?

   Answer: _____

C Explain how you found the answer to **part B.**

Read the problem. Write your answer for each part.

2. A small town has a number of kiosks, or vending machines, that rent movie DVDs. The circle graph below shows the breakdown by type of the movies rented last month. A total of 1,164 action movies were rented.

MOVIE TYPES RENTED

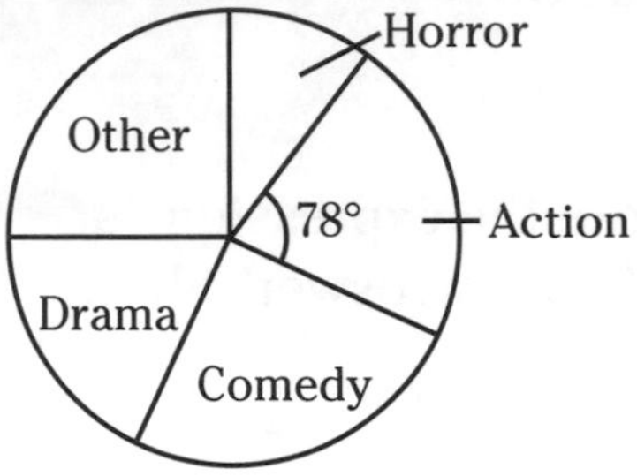

A Approximately what fraction of movies rented last month were action movies?

Answer: _____

B Estimate the total number of all movies rented last month.

Answer: _____

Unit 2 Operations with Real Numbers and Expressions, Part 2

C The company that owns the vending machines has a total
of 29,698 kiosks nationwide. Each week an average of
9.568 million movies are rented from the kiosks.

Estimate the average number of movies rented from a kiosk in
a year.

Answer: _____

D Explain how you found your answer to **part C.**

Read the problem. Write your answer for each part.

3. A manufacturer makes rectangular blankets in several styles and sizes. The outline of a popular blanket in size A is shown below.

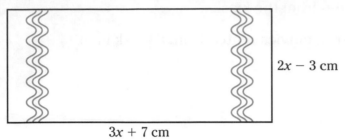

$2x - 3$ cm

$3x + 7$ cm

A Write a polynomial expression, in simplified form, that represents the perimeter of the blanket.

Answer: _____

B Write a polynomial expression, in simplified form, that represents the area of the blanket.

Answer: _____

C The same style blanket in size B has width $2x + 10$ and length $4x - 10$.

Write a polynomial expression, in simplified form, that expresses the difference in area of the blankets A and B. Show all your work.

Answer: _____

Read the problem. Write your answer for each part.

4. A physicist needs to know the values of x for which the trinomial below equals zero. Her first step is to factor the trinomial.

$$x^2 + 10x + 24$$

A Factor the trinomial.

Answer: _____

B Explain how you found your answer to **part A.**

C The physicist also needs to factor the trinomial below.

$$x^2 - 10x + 24$$

What is the factored form of the trinomial?

Answer: _____

D The physicist must factor several trinomials that are all of the form $x^2 - mx + n$, where m and n are whole numbers greater than zero. She wonders if any of these trinomials factor as $(x + a)(x + b)$, where $a > 0$ and $b < 0$. Is that possible? Explain why or why not.

Read the problem. Write your answer for each part.

5. A manufacturing company uses the expressions below to estimate revenue and expenses based on the production of n units.

$$\text{Revenue: } 20n^2 - 180$$

$$\text{Expenses: } 4n^2 + 36n + 72$$

The ratio of revenue to expenses is given by the rational expression below.

$$\frac{20n^2 - 180}{4n^2 + 36n + 72}$$

A Factor the numerator and denominator of the rational expression, and simplify if possible. Show your work.

Answer: _____

B The rational expression $\frac{20n^2 - 180}{4n^2 + 36n + 72}$ is not defined for any values of n for which the denominator equals zero. Find the values of n for which the denominator equals zero.

Answer: _____

C The company accountant says that the rational expression $\frac{20n^2 - 180}{4n^2 + 36n + 72}$ will never have a zero denominator because n, the number of units, is always a whole number. Explain why the accountant is correct.

Module 1
Operations and Linear Equations & Inequalities

Unit 3
Linear Equations

Lesson 1   Linear Equations, Part 1   A1.1.2.1.1, A1.1.2.1.2

Lesson 2   Linear Equations, Part 2   A1.1.2.1.1, A1.1.2.1.2, A1.1.2.1.3

Lesson 3   Systems of Linear Equations   A1.1.2.2.1, A1.1.2.2.2

Unit 3 Constructed-Response Review

Linear Equations, Part 1

A1.1.2.1.1, A1.1.2.1.2

Linear Equations

Real-world patterns and relationships are often modeled by linear equations and represented as straight lines on a graph. A **linear equation** is any equation that includes constants and variables that are multiplied by coefficients. By working with linear equations, you will be able to understand many patterns and relationships in the real world.

The following are all examples of linear equations:

$2x - 12 = 10$

$x + y = \pi$ (Remember that π is just a constant.)

$5x - 4 = \text{-}3x$

The following are *not* examples of linear equations:

$2x^2 - 12 = 10$ (not linear because the variable is squared)

$x + |y| = \pi$ (not linear because one of the variables is inside absolute value symbols)

$\sqrt{5x - 4} = \text{-}3x$ (not linear because the first instance of x is under a square root sign)

An equation is a mathematical statement that two expressions are equal. For example, $7y = 4$ and $3(x - 2) = 8x + 1$ are equations. To write an equation to model a real-life situation, you need to translate a verbal description into mathematical expressions that are set equal to each other.

Try this sample question.

S-1 A tree was 4 feet tall when it was planted. It grows 2 feet a year. Which equation could be solved to find how many years the tree will take to grow to a height of 16 feet from the time it was planted?

A $16 = 4y + 2$

B $16 = 2y + 4$

C $4 = \frac{16y}{2}$

D $4 = \frac{16}{2} + y$

In this situation, the unknown value is the number of years it will take the tree to reach 16 feet from the time it was planted. Assign the variable y to the unknown. Each year, the tree grows 2 feet, or $2y$. Since the tree was already 4 feet tall when it was planted, add 4. The expression $2y + 4$ represents the height after y years. Set this expression equal to 16 for $16 = 2y + 4$. Choice B is correct.

Solving Linear Equations

To solve a linear equation, you need to write it as an equivalent equation with just the variable on the left side. Rewrite the equation by adding, subtracting, multiplying, and dividing, making sure to do the same operation to both sides of the equation. The properties you can use are shown below.

If $x = y$, then:	
$x + a = y + a$	Addition Property of Equality
$x - a = y - a$	Subtraction Property of Equality
$ax = ay$	Multiplication Property of Equality
$\frac{x}{a} = \frac{y}{a}$	Division Property of Equality

For example, here is how to solve the equation $2x - 12 = 10$ for the variable x.

$$2x - 12 = 10$$
$$2x - 12 + 12 = 10 + 12 \qquad \text{Add 12 to both sides of the equation.}$$
$$2x = 22 \qquad \text{Simplify.}$$
$$2x \div 2 = 22 \div 2 \qquad \text{Divide both sides of the equation by 2.}$$
$$x = 11 \qquad \text{Simplify.}$$

Try this sample question.

S-2 What value of x makes the equation below true?

$$3x + 1 = \text{-}23$$

A -8   B -6   C 6   D 8

The original equation is $3x + 1 = \text{-}23$. Subtract 1 from each side and simplify. This results in $3x = \text{-}24$. Next, divide each side by 3 and simplify. This results in $x = \text{-}8$. Choice A is correct.

Often an equation needs to be simplified before it can be solved. Use the properties of numbers and the order of operations to write an equivalent equation. To simplify an equation, you may need to

- **remove parentheses** with the distributive property
- **collect like terms** with the associative or commutative properties
- **isolate the variable** on one side of the equation using properties of equality

Try this sample question.

S-3 What value of x makes the equation below true?

$$4x - (3x - 5) = 2x + 11$$

To find the value of x in this equation, first simplify the left side of the equation. Then combine variable terms onto one side, as shown in the steps below:

$4x - (3x - 5) = 2x + 11$	
$4x - 3x + 5 = 2x + 11$	Distribute -1 to eliminate parentheses.
$x + 5 = 2x + 11$	Combine like terms.
$5 = x + 11$	Subtract x from both sides.
$-6 = x$	Subtract 11 from both sides.

When $x = -6$, the equation is true.

IT'S YOUR TURN

Read each problem. Circle the letter of the best answer.

1. Three friends share the cost of a pizza. The base price of the pizza is p and the extra toppings cost $4.50. If each person's share was $7.15, which equation could be used to find p, the base price of the pizza?

   A $7.15 = 3p - 4.5$

   B $7.15 = \frac{1}{3}p + 4.5$

   C $7.15 = 3(p + 4.5)$

   D $7.15 = \frac{1}{3}(p + 4.5)$

2. What is the solution to the linear equation $-6z + 1 = 13$?

   A $z = -6$

   B $z = -2$

   C $z = 2$

   D $z = 6$

3. Felix buys a carpet for $230. The price is $3.50 per square foot. If Felix had a special discount coupon for $50 off, which linear equation could be used to find the area, A, of the carpet?

   A $230 = 3.5A + 50$

   B $50 = 3.5A - 230$

   C $230 = 3.5A - 50$

   D $50 = 230 - 3.5A$

Read each problem. Circle the letter of the best answer.

4. Lia uses the equation below to estimate the amount of taxes, T, she owes to the government.

$$T = 0.15(d - 7,550) + 755$$

Lia estimates that she owes the government $3,455 in taxes. What is d, the total dollars Lia earned during the past year?

A $15,755

B $20,550

C $25,550

D $30,755

5. The steps Derek used to solve an equation are shown below.

Solve: $0.4x + 5 + 0.2x = 17$

Step 1: $0.4x + 0.2x + 5 = 17$
Step 2: $0.6x + 5 = 17$
Step 3: $0.6x = 12$
Step 4: $x = 20$

Which properties justify Step 1 and Step 3?

A Step 1: Distributive Property
   Step 3: Division Property of Equality

B Step 1: Distributive Property
   Step 3: Subtraction Property of Equality

C Step 1: Commutative Property of Addition
   Step 3: Division Property of Equality

D Step 1: Commutative Property of Addition
   Step 3: Subtraction Property of Equality

6. A restaurant meal for a group of people cost $85 total. This amount included a 6% tax and an 18% tip, both based on the price of the food. Which equation could be used to find f, the cost of the food?

A $85 = 0.24c$

B $85 = 1.06f + 0.18$

C $85 = f + 0.24$

D $85 = 1.24f$

7. What is the solution to the linear equation $\frac{3}{4}y - 5 = 10$?

A $y = \frac{15}{4}$

B $y = \frac{20}{3}$

C $y = \frac{45}{4}$

D $y = 20$

8. A tilesetter is joining two tiles to make a 90° angle. The degree measure of tile A can be represented as $3y + 2$ and of tile B as $5y$. Which equation below is **not** a step in finding the size of each angle?

A $88 = 8y - 2$

B $90 = 8y + 2$

C $\frac{1}{8} \cdot 88 = \frac{1}{8} \cdot 8y$

D $90 = 3y + 2 + 5y$

Read each problem. Circle the letter of the best answer.

9. Tara is solving an equation. Her first step is shown below.

    Solve: $4y - 8(y - 2) = 6$

    Step 1: $4y - 8y + 16 = 6$

    Which property justifies Tara's first step?

    A Identity Property

    B Distributive Property

    C Subtraction Property of Equality

    D Associative Property of Multiplication

10. One-fourth the distance between two cities is 100 miles less than two-thirds the distance between the cities. Which equation expresses this situation?

    A $\frac{1}{4}d - 100 = \frac{2}{3}d$

    B $\frac{1}{4}d = \frac{2}{3}d - 100$

    C $\frac{1}{4}d = \frac{2}{3}d + 100$

    D $\frac{1}{4}d - \frac{2}{3}d = 100$

11. Which is a correct step in solving the following equation for g?

    $$-1.75 + 2(2 - g) = 0$$

    A $2(2 - g) = -1.75$

    B $4 - g = 1.75$

    C $-2g = 1.75 - 4$

    D $g = -2.25 \div 2$

12. Arturo is going to solve this equation.

    $$\frac{5}{8}(x - 4) = \frac{3}{4}(x + 2)$$

    Which statement best describes a correct strategy for the first two steps?

    A 1. Add 4 to both sides using the Addition Property of Equality.
       2. Eliminate the parentheses using the Distributive Property.

    B 1. Add 4 to both sides using the Addition Property of Equality.
       2. Eliminate the parentheses using the Commutative Property.

    C 1. Multiply both sides by 8 using the Multiplication Property of Equality.
       2. Eliminate the parentheses using the Distributive Property.

    D 1. Multiply both sides by 8 using the Multiplication Property of Equality.
       2. Eliminate the parentheses using the Commutative Property.

Linear Equations in Two Variables

If a linear equation has two variables, its solutions are ordered pairs of numbers. For example, $x + y = 6$ is an equation with two variables, and its solutions are all pairs of numbers for x and y like $(0, 6)$, $(2, 4)$, $(3, 3)$, and $(4, 2)$.

To find the solution, first rewrite the equation in an equivalent form with one variable, often y, isolated on the left:

$$x + y = 6$$
$$x + y - x = 6 - x$$
$$y = 6 - x$$

Then substitute a value for x, such as 5, and solve for y.

$$y = 6 - 5$$
$$y = 1$$

One solution for $x + y = 6$ is $(5, 1)$.

Try these sample questions.

S-1 Which equation shows $3x + 5y = 10$ in simplest form in terms of y?

A $y = -\frac{3}{5}x + 2$

B $y = \frac{3}{5}x + 2$

C $y = 2x + \frac{3}{5}$

D $y = 3x + \frac{2}{5}$

To rewrite the equation in terms of y means to isolate y on one side of the equation.

$$3x + 5y = 10$$
$$3x + 5y - 3x = 10 - 3x \qquad \text{Subtract } 3x \text{ from both sides.}$$
$$5y = 10 - 3x \qquad \text{Simplify.}$$
$$\tfrac{1}{5} \cdot 5y = \tfrac{1}{5}(10 - 3x) \qquad \text{Multiply by } \tfrac{1}{5} \text{ or divide by 5.}$$
$$y = \tfrac{1}{5} \cdot 10 - \tfrac{1}{5} \cdot 3x \qquad \text{Distribute } \tfrac{1}{5}.$$
$$y = 2 - \tfrac{3}{5}x \qquad \text{Simplify.}$$
$$y = -\tfrac{3}{5}x + 2 \qquad \text{Reorder using the commutative law.}$$

Choice A is correct.

S-2 What is the value of y in the following equation when $x = 9$?

$$\frac{2}{3}x - y = -4$$

A -10 **B** -7.5 **C** 7.5 **D** 10

Start by substituting 9 for the value of x: $\frac{2}{3}(9) - y = -4$. Simplify the equation to $6 - y = -4$. Isolate y by subtracting 6 from both sides: $-y = -4 - 6$. Remember that subtraction is the same as adding the opposite: $-y = -4 + (-6)$, so $-y = -10$. Now use the property of -1 to multiply both sides and change the signs: $(-1)(-y) = (-1)(10)$ results in $y = 10$. Choice D is correct.

Interpreting Solutions to Linear Equations

The ordered pairs that make up the solutions to a linear equation have specific meanings in the context of a real-world problem. To understand the meanings of the x- and y-values, look back at the situation described in the problem and decide what the variables represent.

Try this sample question.

S-3 Jane spent $10 at the ice cream truck. She bought x ice cream cones and y sundaes. The equation below shows the relationship between the number of ice cream cones and the number of sundaes she bought.

$$3x + 4y = 10$$

The ordered pair $(2, 1)$ is a solution of the equation. What does the solution $(2, 1)$ represent?

A Sundaes cost $2 each and ice cream cones cost $1 each.

B A sundae costs 2 times as much as an ice cream cone.

C Jane spent $2 on sundaes and $1 on ice cream cones.

D Jane bought 2 ice cream cones and 1 sundae.

Reread the problem and note the way x and y are used in relation to the nouns: "x ice cream cones and y sundaes" indicates numbers of ice cream cones and sundaes. Choice D is correct.

Read each problem. Circle the letter of the best answer.

1. Jackson has 75¢ in dimes, *d,* and nickels, *n,* in his pocket. Which equation could be solved to find the possible combinations of dimes and nickels Jackson has?

   A $75 = d + n$

   B $75 = dn$

   C $75 = 10d \cdot 5n$

   D $75 = 10d + 5n$

2. The linear equation below has two variables.

   $$y = -\frac{1}{4}x - 1$$

   Which shows the solutions to the equation when $x = 4$, $x = 0$, and $x = -4$?

   A $(-2, 4), (1, 0), (0, -4)$

   B $(4, -2), (0, -1), (-4, 0)$

   C $(2, -4), (-1, 0), (0, 4)$

   D $(-4, 2), (0, 1), (4, 0)$

3. A 50-foot roll of fencing will be used to enclose a rectangular garden. Which equation below could **not** be solved to find the possible lengths, *l,* and widths, *w,* of the garden?

   A $50 = 2lw$

   B $\frac{50}{2} = l + w$

   C $2(l + w) = 50$

   D $50 = 2l + 2w$

4. Ms. Monti bought *x* adult tickets and *y* children's tickets to an ice-skating show. She spent a total of $145. The equation below describes the relationship between *x* and *y.*

   $$25x + 15y = 145$$

   The ordered pair $(4, 3)$ is a solution of the equation. What does the solution $(4, 3)$ represent?

   A Ms. Monti bought 4 adult tickets and 3 children's tickets.

   B Adult tickets cost $4 each and children's tickets cost $3 each.

   C Ms. Monti spent $4 on adult tickets and $3 on children's tickets.

   D The cost of 4 adult tickets equals the cost of 3 children's tickets.

5. Look at the linear equation below.

   $$-1.5x - 10y = 5$$

   What is the value of *y* when $x = 6$?

   A 1.4

   B 0.9

   C –0.9

   D –1.4

Read each problem. Circle the letter of the best answer.

6. The growth of a kitten is described by the equation $y = 2.5x + 4$, where y represents the kitten's weight in ounces x weeks after it was born. What is the meaning of the fact that the point $(4, 14)$ lies on the graph of the equation?

   A The kitten had an initial weight of 4 ounces.

   B The kitten is growing at a rate of 4 ounces per week.

   C The kitten weighed 4 ounces when it was 14 weeks old.

   D The kitten weighed 14 ounces when it was 4 weeks old.

7. Jorge earns $12 an hour. Deductions for taxes and insurance take 25% of his earnings. Which equation could be solved to find Jorge's take-home pay, p, after h hours of work?

   A $p = 12h - 0.25$

   B $p - 0.25h = 12h$

   C $p = (0.75)12h$

   D $p = (12 - 0.25)h$

8. Look at the linear equation below.

   $$2x - 3y = -13$$

   Which pair of numbers is a solution to the equation?

   A $(-5, -1)$

   B $(-5, 1)$

   C $(5, -1)$

   D $(5, 1)$

9. For which linear equation below is $(-7.5, -2.5)$ a solution?

   A $y = -3x$

   B $y = -\frac{1}{3}x$

   C $y = 3x$

   D $y = \frac{1}{3}x$

10. The lengths in inches $(x$ and $y)$ of two fish are related by the equation $5x - 4y = 24$. The two ordered pairs below are solutions to the equation.

    $$(4, -1) \qquad (12, 9)$$

    Which statement best evaluates whether these two solutions make sense in this situation?

    A Both solutions make sense in this situation.

    B Neither solution makes sense in this situation.

    C The solution $(4, -1)$ makes sense in this situation, but $(12, 9)$ does not.

    D The solution $(12, 9)$ makes sense in this situation, but $(4, -1)$ does not.

Systems of Linear Equations

A1.1.2.2.1, A1.1.2.2.2

Many real-world situations are described by linear equations, whose graphs are straight lines. In many problem-solving situations, it is important to determine where, if at all, two straight lines intersect. The point of intersection usually has special significance in the context of the problem.

Solving Systems of Equations by Graphing

Graphing is one way the point of intersection can be found for a system involving two equations of straight lines.

Consider the system of equations below.

> A **system of linear equations** is a set of two or more linear equations that must be solved at the same time.

$$\begin{cases} y = x + 4 \\ y = 2x \end{cases}$$

Each equation, by itself, has an infinite number of solutions. For example, the points $(0, 4)$, $(1, 5)$, and $(2, 6)$ are just a few of the solutions to the first equation. However, when solving a system of two equations, you are looking for points that satisfy *both* equations at the same time.

To solve this system, graph both equations on the same coordinate plane.

It is easy to see from the graph that the lines intersect at the point $(4, 8)$. You can check that this is correct by substituting $x = 4$ and $y = 8$ into each equation to show that both equations are true.

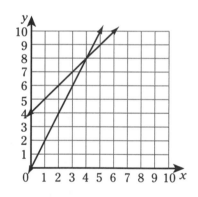

$$y = x + 4 \qquad y = 2x$$
$$8 = 4 + 4 \checkmark \qquad 8 = 2(4) \checkmark$$

Try this sample question.

S-1 Marnie needs to print posters for a community event. Stellar Printers will charge Marnie a $300 set-up fee plus $1 per poster. Artemis Printers will charge Marnie a $200 set-up fee plus $1.50 per poster.

   A Write a system of equations that relates the total cost at each company to the number of posters printed.

   B Solve your system of equations by using the graphing method.

   C Explain what the solution to your system of equations represents in the context of the problem.

For part A, the printing costs for the two companies can be modeled by this system of equations, where y is the cost in dollars and x is the number of posters.

$$\begin{cases} y = 300 + 1.00x \text{ (Stellar Printers)} \\ y = 200 + 1.50x \text{ (Artemis Printers)} \end{cases}$$

For part B, graph both of these equations to find where they intersect. A graph is shown below.

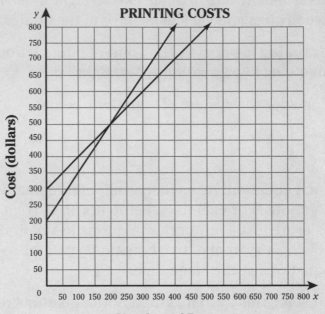

Look at the graph to see where the two lines intersect: $(200, 500)$. This point is the solution to the system of equations.

For part C, it means that both companies will charge Marnie the same amount of money, $500, to print 200 posters.

Solving Systems of Equations Using Substitution

Using algebra techniques, such as **substitution,** is another way systems of equations can be solved. Follow these steps when solving systems of equations using substitution:

1. Solve at least one equation for either x or y.

2. Substitute the resulting expression for the variable it equals in the other equation.

3. Solve the equation.

4. Substitute the value of the variable found in step 3 into either original equation to find the value of the other variable.

Try this sample question.

S-2 What is the solution to the system of equations below?

$$\begin{cases} -x + y = 40 \\ y = 5x + 80 \end{cases}$$

A $(10, 50)$ B $(-10, 30)$ C $(30, 10)$ D $(30, 70)$

The second equation is already set equal to y. Substitute the expression $5x + 80$ for y into the first equation. Then solve the resulting equation for x.

$-x + y = 40$	
$-x + (5x + 80) = 40$	Substitute expression for y.
$4x + 80 = 40$	Combine variable terms.
$4x = -40$	Subtract 80 from each side.
$x = -10$	Divide each side by 4.
$-(-10) + y = 40$	Substitute -10 for x into the first equation.
$10 + y = 40$	Simplify.
$y = 30$	Subtract 10 from each side.

The solution to the system of equations is $x = -10$ and $y = 30$. Choice B is correct.

Solving Systems of Equations Using Elimination

A second method used for solving systems of equations algebraically is known as **elimination.** With the elimination method, equations are added or subtracted to eliminate one of the variables, making it possible to solve for the remaining variable.

To solve the system below, you can simply add the two equations. The y-terms cancel out, and then you can solve for x:

$$\begin{array}{l} x + y = 3 \\ \underline{2x - y = 3} \\ 3x \quad\;\; = 6 \\ \quad x = 2 \end{array}$$ (Notice that $+ y$ added to $- y$ equals 0.)

Then find y by substituting $x = 2$ in either one of the original equations:

$$\begin{array}{l} x + y = 3 \\ 2 + y = 3 \\ \quad y = 1 \end{array}$$

So the solution is $x = 2$ and $y = 1$, or simply $(2, 1)$.

Try this sample question.

S-3 What is the solution to the system of equations shown below?

$$\begin{cases} 4x - y = 7 \\ -4x - 2y = 2 \end{cases}$$

A $(-1, 3)$ B $(1, -3)$ C $(2, -3)$ D $(3, 5)$

Adding these equations causes the x-terms to cancel out, resulting in $-3y = 9$, which means $y = -3$. Substituting $y = -3$ in the first equation, and solving for x, you get: $4x - (-3) = 7 \rightarrow 4x = 4 \rightarrow x = 1$. So the solution is $(1, -3)$. Choice B is correct.

Solving Systems of Equations Using Multiplication

To solve a system of equations, sometimes you must multiply one or both equations by an appropriate number before you add the two equations. Look at this example:

$$\begin{cases} x + 2y = 5 \\ 3x + 3y = 6 \end{cases}$$

Simply adding these equations will not cause either the x-terms or the y-terms to cancel out. But if you multiply both sides of the first equation by -3, then add the equations, the x-terms will cancel out:

$$\begin{array}{ll} (-3)(x + 2y) = (5)(-3) \\ \underline{3x + 3y = 6} \end{array} \rightarrow \begin{array}{l} -3x - 6y = -15 \\ \underline{3x + 3y = 6} \\ -3y = -9 \\ y = 3 \end{array}$$

Substitute $y = 3$ in one of the original two equations and solve for x:

$$\begin{array}{r} x + 2y = 5 \\ x + 2(3) = 5 \\ x + 6 = 5 \\ x = -1 \end{array}$$

So the solution is $(-1, 3)$. In other words, the lines $x + 2y = 5$ and $3x + 3y = 6$ both contain the point $(-1, 3)$.

Try this sample question.

S-4 What is the solution to the system of equations shown below?

$$\begin{cases} x - 4y = 9 \\ 2x + 3y = -4 \end{cases}$$

A $(1, -4)$ B $(1, -2)$ C $(5, -1)$ D $(7, -6)$

To find the *x*-terms that cancel, multiply the first equation by -2. Then add to get rid of the *x*-terms. Solving for *y*, you should get $y = -2$. Then substitute $y = -2$ into one of the original equations to get $x = 1$. So the solution is $(1, -2)$. Choice B is correct.

When two lines are graphed on the same coordinate system, there are three possibilities:

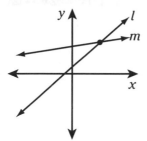

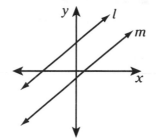

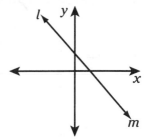

Two lines that intersect in 1 point — One solution to the system of equations

Two lines that do not intersect (parallel lines) — No solution to the system of equations

Two identical lines — Infinite number of solutions to the system of equations

The following example shows a system with no solution.

$$\begin{cases} x - 2y = 4 \\ -x + 2y = 7 \end{cases} \qquad \begin{array}{l} x - 2y = 4 \\ \underline{-x + 2y = 7} \\ 0 = 11 \end{array}$$

Since $0 = 11$ is never true, this system has no solution. The lines described by the equations $x - 2y = 4$ and $-x + 2y = 7$ are parallel.

The next example shows a system with an infinite number of solutions.

$$\begin{cases} -4x - 6y = -10 \\ 4x + 6y = 10 \end{cases} \qquad \begin{array}{l} -4x - 6y = -10 \\ \underline{4x + 6y = 10} \\ 0 = 0 \end{array}$$

Since $0 = 0$ is always true, this system has an infinite number of solutions. The equations $-4x - 6y = -10$ and $4x + 6y = 10$ describe the same line.

Read each problem. Circle the letter of the best answer.

1. What is the solution to the system of equations graphed below?

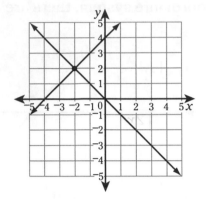

   A $(-4, 0)$

   B $(-2, 2)$

   C $(0, 0)$

   D $(0, 4)$

2. Look at this system of equations.

$$\begin{cases} y = 2x - 1 \\ 4x + y = 2 \end{cases}$$

   Which shows a correct step in using substitution to solve the system of equations?

   A $4x + y = 2x - 1$

   B $4x + 2x - 1 = 2$

   C $6x - 2 = y$

   D $6x + 2 = 2y$

3. What is the solution to the system of equations shown below?

$$\begin{cases} 2x + 2y = 12 \\ 6x - 2y = 20 \end{cases}$$

   A $(0, 6)$

   B $(2, 2)$

   C $(3, 3)$

   D $(4, 2)$

4. A new company's expenses and income are graphed below.

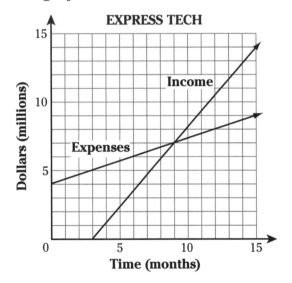

   When did the company start to make as much money as it spent?

   A 3 months

   B 4 months

   C 9 months

   D 16 months

Read each problem. Circle the letter of the best answer.

5. Dani bought a total of 8 pounds of peanuts and cashews. Peanuts, p, cost $2 per pound and cashews, c, cost $5 per pound. The total amount Dani spent on the peanuts and cashews was $25. Which system of equations could be solved to find how many pounds of peanuts Dani bought?

   A $\begin{cases} 2p + 5c = 25 \\ p + c = 8 \end{cases}$

   B $\begin{cases} 5p + 2c = 25 \\ p + c = 8 \end{cases}$

   C $\begin{cases} 2p + 5c = 8 \\ p + c = 25 \end{cases}$

   D $\begin{cases} 2p = 8 \\ 5c = 25 \end{cases}$

6. Study the system of equations below.

   $$\begin{cases} x + y = -4 \\ x - y = 10 \end{cases}$$

   What is the solution to the system of equations?

   A $(-4, 10)$

   B $(10, 4)$

   C $(3, -7)$

   D $(7, -3)$

7. A postage stamp is shaped like a rectangle with a perimeter of 88 millimeters. The length (x) is 10 millimeters less than twice the width (y). The system of equations shown below represents this situation.

   $$\begin{cases} x = 2y - 10 \\ 2x + 2y = 88 \end{cases}$$

   Which statement is true?

   A The width of the stamp is 12 millimeters.

   B The length of the stamp is 36 millimeters.

   C The width of the stamp is 8 millimeters less than the length.

   D The length of the stamp is 10 millimeters greater than the width.

8. What is the y-value of the solution to the system of equations shown below?

   $$\begin{cases} 5x + 4y = 12 \\ -5x - 2y = -16 \end{cases}$$

   A -4

   B -2

   C 2

   D 4

Read the problem. Circle the letter of the best answer.

9. Look at the system of equations below.

$$\begin{cases} y = x + 2 \\ y = 2x - 3 \end{cases}$$

Which coordinate plane shows the solution to this system of equations?

A

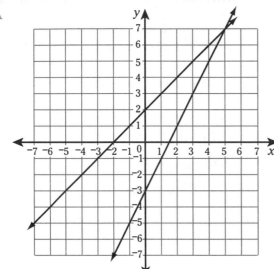

C

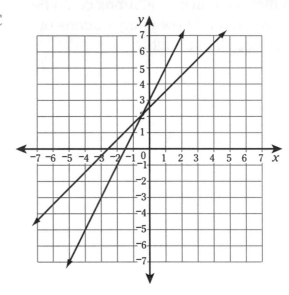

B

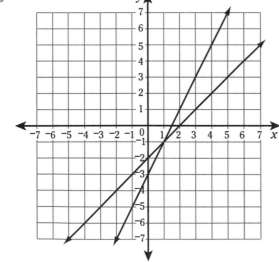

D

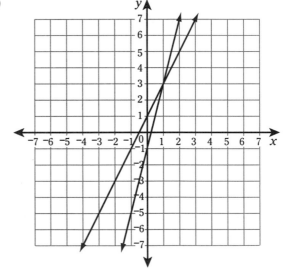

Read each problem. Circle the letter of the best answer.

10. Nathan mixed x quarts of milk containing 2% fat with y quarts of milk containing 4% fat. The total amount of the mixture was 9 quarts, and it contained a total of 0.24 quart of fat. This situation is represented by the system of equations shown below.

$$\begin{cases} x + y = 9 \\ 0.02x + 0.04y = 0.24 \end{cases}$$

Which statement is true?

A Nathan used twice as much 2% milk as 4% milk.

B Nathan used twice as much 4% milk as 2% milk.

C Nathan used 2 quarts more 2% milk than 4% milk.

D Nathan used 2 quarts more 4% milk than 2% milk.

11. Mr. Santana is 3 times his daughter Kara's age. Ten years ago, Mr. Santana was 7 times Kara's age. Which system of equations could you solve to find Mr. Santana's current age?

A $\begin{cases} 3f = d \\ f - 10 = 7d - 10 \end{cases}$

B $\begin{cases} f = 3d \\ f + 10 = 7(d + 10) \end{cases}$

C $\begin{cases} f = \dfrac{d}{3} \\ f + 10 = 7d - 10 \end{cases}$

D $\begin{cases} f = 3d \\ f - 10 = 7(d - 10) \end{cases}$

12. Molly is selling bracelets and necklaces at a craft fair. The cost of 4 bracelets and 3 necklaces is $23.50. The cost of 5 bracelets and 2 necklaces is $21.50. The system of equations shown below represents this situation.

$$\begin{cases} 4b + 3n = 23.50 \\ 5b + 2n = 21.50 \end{cases}$$

A customer bought 1 bracelet and 1 necklace. How much money did the customer spend?

A $6.50

B $7.00

C $7.50

D $8.00

Read the problem. Write your answer for each part.

1. Vic and Eva buy used cars at the same time. Vic buys a car with 10,000 miles on it. He drives an average of 100 miles a week. The equation below can be used to determine how many miles, m, will be on the car after any number of weeks of driving, w.

$$m = 100w + 10,000$$

A In how many weeks will Vic's car have 12,000 miles on it?

Answer: _____

Eva buys a car with 7,000 miles on it. She drives an average of 400 miles a week.

B Use the system of equations below to find in how many weeks Vic's and Eva's cars will have the same number of miles on them.

$$\begin{cases} m = 100w + 10,000 \\ m = 400w + 7,000 \end{cases}$$

Answer: _____

C How many miles, *m,* will the cars have on them when the number of weeks, *w,* is the same? Use the system of equations from **part B.** Show how you found your answer.

Answer: _____

Read the problem. Write your answer for each part.

2. Padma rented a bike for x hours and a kayak for y hours while she was on vacation.

   A She rented the bike and kayak for a total of 7 hours. Write an equation to represent this situation.

   Answer: _____

   The bike cost $6 an hour and the kayak cost $10 an hour. Padma spent a total of $60 for the bike and kayak rentals.

   B Write an equation to represent this situation.

   Answer: _____

C How many hours did Padma rent the kayak? Show or explain
your work.

Answer: _____

Read the problem. Write your answer for each part.

3. The table shows how the length of Alex's pet lizard is changing over time.

PET LIZARD GROWTH

Age (years)	Length (centimeters)
1	5.0
2	7.4
3	9.8
4	12.2
5	14.6

A Write an equation using x and y to find the length of the lizard based on its age.

Answer: _____

B Describe what the x and y variables represent in your equation.

C Use your equation to predict the length of the lizard when it is
   12 years old. Show your work.

Answer: _____

Read the problem. Write your answer for each part.

4. Rosalina has two sizes of bricks to use to build a wall, as shown below.

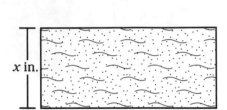
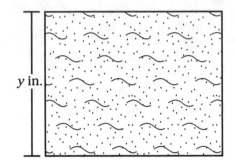

If Rosalina stacks 3 small bricks and 2 large bricks, the total height is 26 inches. If she stacks 5 small bricks and 3 large bricks, the total height is 41 inches. Rosalina wrote the system of equations shown below to represent this situation.

$$\begin{cases} 3x + 2y = 26 \\ 5x + 3y = 41 \end{cases}$$

A To solve the system, Rosalina's first step was to multiply both sides of the first equation by 3. What algebraic property justifies that step?

Answer: _____

B Complete Rosalina's work and solve the system of equations. Show and explain each step of your work.

C Explain what the solution to the system of equations means in this situation.

Read the problem. Write your answer for each part.

5. Ms. Chen is buying a printer for her computer. She needs to choose between two different brands, the Voltroxx printer and the Inkwest printer. For whichever printer she buys, she will also need to buy ink cartridges. Information about the two printers is shown in the table below.

PRINTER COMPARISON

Brand of Printer	Cost of Printer	Cost of Ink Cartridges
Voltroxx	$50	$30 each
Inkwest	$80	$27 each

A Write a system of linear equations that relates Ms. Chen's total cost to the number of cartridges needed.

Answer: _____

B What is the solution to this system of equations? Show your work.

Answer: _____

C What does the solution to this system of equations represent in the context of the problem?

Module 1
Operations and Linear Equations & Inequalities

Unit 4
Linear Inequalities

Linear Inequalities

A1.1.3.1.2, A1.1.3.1.3

Linear Inequalities

A **linear inequality** is similar to a linear equation, but the equals sign is replaced by an inequality sign. For example, $-2x \leq 5$ and $5y + 2 > 0$ are linear inequalities. With a linear equation in one variable, there is one solution. A linear inequality, however, has a range of solutions, called the **solution set.**

> $<$ means "is less than"
> $>$ means "is greater than"
> $\leq$ means "is less than or equal to"
> $\geq$ means "is greater than or equal to"

Solving Linear Inequalities

Linear inequalities are solved much the same way as linear equations. The properties that justify each step in the solution of an equation or inequality are given on page 63 of this book.

The steps used in solving the inequality $5(x + 2) > 6$ are shown below.

Step	Statement	Reason
1	$5(x + 2) > 6$	Given
2	$5x + 10 > 6$	Distributive Property
3	$5x > -4$	Subtraction Property of Equality
4	$x > -\dfrac{4}{5}$	Division Property of Equality

Try this sample question.

S-1 What is the solution to the inequality $3x - 9 \geq 6$?

  A $x \geq -9$ **B** $x \geq -1$ **C** $x \geq 5$ **D** $x \geq 45$

> Choice C is correct. Adding 9 to each side gives the inequality $3x \geq 15$. Dividing each side gives the solution $x \geq 5$. In other words, any value of x greater than or equal to 5 makes the inequality $3x - 9 \geq 6$ true.

An important difference between solving linear equations and solving linear inequalities is this:

- When multiplying or dividing by a negative number, the direction of the inequality symbol *must* be changed.

Try this sample question.

S-2 What is the solution to the inequality $-\dfrac{y}{5} + 6 > 2$?

  A $y < -20$ **B** $y < 20$ **C** $y > -20$ **D** $y > 20$

Unit 4 Linear Inequalities

Choice B is correct. First subtract 6 from each side, giving the inequality $-\frac{y}{5} > -4$. Then multiply each side by -5 and reverse the inequality sign, and the solution is $y < 20$.

Graphs of Linear Inequalities

When an inequality involves only a single variable, its solution may be graphed on a number line. Some examples are given below.

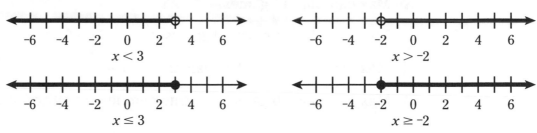

Open circles are used to symbolize the $<$ and $>$ signs; an open circle means the number is *not* part of the solution set. Closed circles are used to symbolize the $\leq$ and $\geq$ signs; a closed circle means the number *is* part of the solution set.

Try this sample question.

S-3 Which graph represents the solution set for the inequality shown below?

$$9 - 2x \geq 1$$

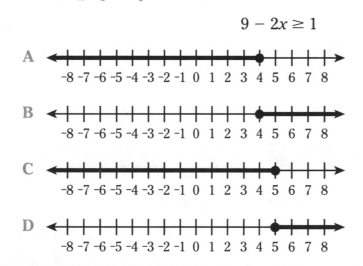

Solve the inequality using these steps:

$$9 - 2x \geq 1$$

$-2x \geq -8$ Subtract 9 from both sides.

$x \leq 4$ Divide both sides by -2.

Change the direction of the inequality symbol.

Choice A is correct.

Interpreting Solutions to Inequalities

Some word problems must be solved using an inequality. If the inequality is not given, you must be able to write one using the given information and then solve it in the context of the problem.

S-4 Max brought $20.00 to the arcade. Each arcade game costs $1.25 to play. He used $6.50 of his money to buy snacks. What is the greatest number of arcade games Max can play with the money he has left?

   A Max can play 11 games.

   B Max can play at most 10 games.

   C Max can play at least 10 games.

   D Max can play 10 games but this number is neither the most nor least.

Write an inequality to find the number of arcade games, *a*, Max can play. The amount paid for snacks plus the amount spent on arcade games should not be more than $20.00:

$$6.50 + 1.25a \leq 20.00$$

$$1.25a \leq 13.50 \quad \text{Subtract 6.50 from both sides.}$$

$$a \leq 10.8 \quad \text{Divide both sides by 1.25. Remember that the direction of the inequality symbol does } \textit{not} \text{ change when dividing by a positive number.}$$

The number of games must be a whole number. Since Max doesn't have quite enough money to play 11 games, the most he can play is 10 games. Choice B is correct.

IT'S YOUR TURN

Read each problem. Circle the letter of the best answer.

1. The solution set of an inequality is graphed on the number line below.

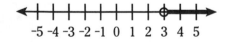
-5 -4 -3 -2 -1 0 1 2 3 4 5

The graph shows the solution set for which inequality?

   A $8x - 16 > 8$

   B $8x + 16 > 8$

   C $8x - 16 < 8$

   D $8x + 16 < 8$

2. Which of the following graphs shows the solution to the inequality $\frac{2}{3}y + 2 \leq 3$?

   A

   B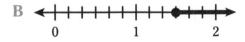

   C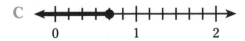

   D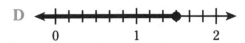

Unit 4 Linear Inequalities

Read each problem. Circle the letter of the best answer.

3. Madison has a goal of saving more than $1,000. She has $300 saved now, and each month she adds $40 to that amount. The inequality $40m + 300 > 1,000$ can be solved to find the number of months, m, it will take Madison to reach her goal. Which statement about the number of months it will take Madison to reach her goal is true?

   A It will take less than 17 months for Madison to reach her goal.

   B Madison will reach her goal in 17 months.

   C Madison will reach her goal in 18 months.

   D It will take more than 18 months for Madison to reach her goal.

4. Which of the following graphs shows the solution to the inequality $-\frac{1}{2}x - 4 < 0$?

   A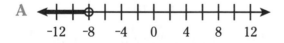
   -12   -8   -4   0   4   8   12

   B ![number line]
   -12   -8   -4   0   4   8   12

   C ![number line]
   -12   -8   -4   0   4   8   12

   D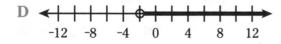
   -12   -8   -4   0   4   8   12

5. The solution set of an inequality is graphed on the number line below.

   -8 -7 -6 -5 -4 -3 -2 -1 0 1 2 3 4 5 6 7 8

   The graph shows the solution set for which inequality?

   A $6x - 4(3x - 2) \le 20$

   B $-6x - 4(3x - 2) \le 20$

   C $6x - 4(3x - 2) \ge 20$

   D $-6x - 4(3x - 2) \ge 20$

6. Ellis can spend up to $40 for gasoline and a carwash at a service station. The carwash will cost $6.00, and gasoline costs $4.50 per gallon. The inequality below can be solved for g, the number of gallons of gasoline Ellis can buy.

   $$4.5g + 6 \le 40$$

   Which of the following is a true statement?

   A Ellis can buy over 10 gallons of gasoline.

   B Ellis can buy at most 7 gallons of gasoline.

   C Ellis can buy 6 gallons of gasoline, but not 7 gallons.

   D Ellis can buy 7 gallons of gasoline, but not 8 gallons.

Read each problem. Circle the letter of the best answer.

7. Which graph shows the solution to the inequality $-2x - 7 \geq -3$?

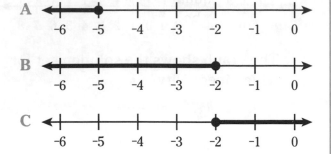

A
-6 -5 -4 -3 -2 -1 0

B
-6 -5 -4 -3 -2 -1 0

C
-6 -5 -4 -3 -2 -1 0

D
-6 -5 -4 -3 -2 -1 0

8. A warehouse elevator can hold at most 1,750 pounds. A 200-pound worker loads the elevator with boxes that weigh 75 pounds each. The inequality $75b + 200 \leq 1,750$ describes the maximum number of boxes the worker can put on the elevator if he is also on the elevator. Which statement is true?

A He can load at least 20 boxes.

B He can load at most 20 boxes.

C He can load at least 21 boxes.

D He can load at most 21 boxes.

9. Which graph shows the solution set to the inequality below?

$$3(3 - k) < -12$$

A
-8 -6 -4 -2 0 2 4 6 8

B
-8 -6 -4 -2 0 2 4 6 8

C
-8 -6 -4 -2 0 2 4 6 8

D
-8 -6 -4 -2 0 2 4 6 8

10. Andre is going to teach a guitar class. There are 11 students signed up so far. Andre charges each student a $45 fee, and he hopes to collect a total of at least $700 in fees. The inequality below can be solved for n, the number of additional students that need to sign up.

$$45(11 + n) \geq 700$$

Which of the following is a true statement?

A The number of additional students needed is 5 or more.

B The number of additional students needed is 10 or more.

C If 5 more students sign up, the total fees will be exactly $700.

D If 4 more students sign up, the total fees will be greater than $700.

Compound Inequalities

Compound Inequalities

A **compound inequality** is formed when two inequalities are joined by the words *and* or *or*. A compound inequality can also be written as a single number sentence with two inequality signs. Examples of such inequalities and their graphs are shown below.

- $n \geq -3$ and $n < 4$, also written as $-3 \leq n < 4$

- $n < 2$ or $n \geq 6$

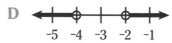

> An open circle on the number line means a number is *not* part of the solution set. A closed circle means the number *is* part of the solution set.

To find the solution to a compound inequality, solve each inequality separately. Sometimes it helps to rewrite inequalities containing *and* as two separate inequalities.

> Remember to change the direction of the inequality symbol when multiplying or dividing by a negative number.

Try this sample question.

S-1 Which graph shows the solution to $7 < -3 - 2x < 11$?

A

C

B

D

Write the compound inequality as two separate inequalities joined by the word *and.* Then solve each inequality.

$$7 < -3 - 2x \quad \text{and} \quad -3 - 2x < 11$$
$$10 < -2x \qquad\qquad -2x < 14 \qquad \text{Add 3 to each side.}$$
$$-5 > x \qquad\qquad\quad x > -7 \qquad \text{Divide each side by -2. Change the direction of each inequality symbol.}$$

Note that $-5 > x$ is the same as $x < -5$. So, x is greater than -7 and less than -5. Choice A is correct.

Absolute Value Inequalities

Recall that expressions inside absolute value symbols can be positive or negative. For example, in the equation $|5p| = 15$, $5p = 15$ or $5p = -15$.

Absolute value inequalities can be solved in a similar manner by setting up two inequalities using the rules described below.

- If $ax + b$ is a variable expression and $c > 0$, then $|ax + b| < c$ can be solved using this compound inequality: $ax + b < c$ *and* $ax + b > -c$.

- If $ax + b$ is a variable expression and $c > 0$, then $|ax + b| > c$ can be solved using this compound inequality: $ax + b > c$ *or* $ax + b < -c$.

Similar rules apply for the inequality symbols $\leq$ and $\geq$.

Notice when the absolute value is *less than c,* the two inequalities are combined using the word *and.* The graph of this solution will cover a closed range of values.

> Two inequalities combined by *and* can be written as one inequality. For example, $x > 2$ *and* $x \leq 7$ is the same as $2 < x \leq 7$.

When the absolute value is *greater than c,* the two inequalities are combined using the word *or.* The graph of this solution will cover an infinite number of solutions in either direction on a number line.

Try this sample question.

S-2 What is the solution to the inequality below?

$$|b + 8| \geq 7$$

A $1 \leq b \leq 15$

B $-1 \leq b \leq 15$

C $b \leq -1$ or $b \geq 15$

D $b \leq -15$ or $b \geq -1$

> Write the absolute value inequality as two separate inequalities. These inequalities are in the form $|ax + b| \geq c$, so use the *or* form of the inequality. Then solve each inequality:
>
> $ax + b \geq c$ or $ax + b \leq -c$
>
> $b + 8 \geq 7$ or $b + 8 \leq -7$
>
> $b \geq -1$ or $b \leq -15$ Subtract 8 from each side.
>
> So, *b* is greater than or equal to -1 or less than or equal to -15. Choice D is correct.

Read each problem. Circle the letter of the best answer.

1. What is the solution to the compound inequality $5 + 3j < 2$ or $2j - 7 > \text{-}3$?

    A $j < \text{-}1$ or $j > 2$

    B $j < 1$ or $j > 2$

    C $j < 1$ or $j > \text{-}5$

    D $j < \text{-}1$ or $j > \text{-}5$

2. Two sides of a triangle are 6 mm and 9 mm long. The possible lengths for the remaining side of the triangle, *s,* can be found using the compound inequality below.

    $$6 + s > 9 \text{ and } 6 + 9 > s$$

    Which graph shows the possible lengths for the remaining side of the triangle?

    A

    B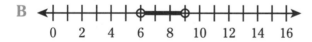

    C

    D

3. A compound inequality is shown below.

    $$2 \leq 5 - 3y \leq 14$$

    What is the solution to the compound inequality?

    A $\text{-}3 \leq y \leq \text{-}1$

    B $\text{-}3 \leq y \leq 1$

    C $\text{-}1 \leq y \leq 3$

    D $1 \leq y \leq 3$

4. Which graph shows the solution to $|2k - 1| < 5$?

    A

    B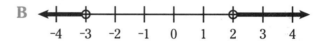

    C

    D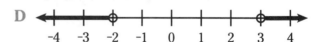

5. What is the solution to the absolute value inequality below?

    $$|5q + 20| > 15$$

    A $\text{-}1 < q < 1$

    B $\text{-}7 < q < \text{-}1$

    C $q < \text{-}1$ or $q > 1$

    D $q < \text{-}7$ or $q > \text{-}1$

Read each problem. Circle the letter of the best answer.

6. In a survey, 61% of the people asked said they would vote yes for the town budget. The margin of error is 2.5%. The inequality $|n - 61| \leq 2.5$ can be used to find the range of voters likely to vote yes for the budget. Which shows the solution to this inequality?

   A $58.5 \leq n \leq 61$

   B $58.5 \leq n \leq 63.5$

   C $61 \leq n \leq 63.5$

   D $2.5 \leq n \leq 63.5$

7. Which graph shows the solution to the absolute value inequality $|4m + 2| \geq 6$?

   A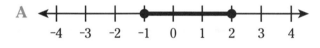

   B

   C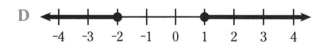

   D

8. The optimal depth for a certain reservoir is between 50 and 60 feet (inclusive). Its depth reached a maximum of 64 feet on March 1st, and then began to decrease at a rate of 0.5 foot per week. The inequality below can be solved for n, the number of weeks after March 1st for which the reservoir will be at optimal depth.

$$50 \leq 64 - 0.5n \leq 60$$

According to this inequality, which of the following is a true statement?

   A The reservoir will be at optimal depth for 20 weeks.

   B The reservoir will not reach optimal depth until October.

   C The reservoir will take over a year to reach optimal depth.

   D The reservoir will be at optimal depth 6 weeks after March 1st.

Systems of Linear Inequalities

A1.1.3.2.1, A1.1.3.2.2

Graphs of Linear Inequalities in Two Variables

When an inequality involves two variables, its solution is best represented on the coordinate plane rather than the number line. Graphing inequalities in two variables is very similar to graphing equations.

Consider the inequality $y - 2x > 1$. By adding $2x$ to both sides, you can rewrite this inequality as $y > 2x + 1$. To graph this inequality, first notice that the inequality is similar to the linear equation $y = 2x + 1$ (shown below), a straight line with a slope of 2 and a y-intercept of 1.

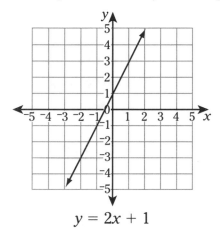

$y = 2x + 1$

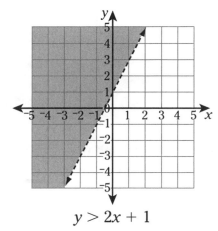

$y > 2x + 1$

The graph of the inequality $y > 2x + 1$ is exactly the area *above* the graph of the line $y = 2x + 1$, as shown in the graph above. To determine which side of the graph is shaded, a test point can be substituted into the original inequality. If that solution is true, the side containing the test point is shaded. Otherwise, the opposite side is shaded. Notice that when the line itself is *not* part of the graph, the line drawn is dashed.

Graphs of inequalities with $\geq$ or $\leq$ include the line.
Graphs of inequalities with $>$ or $<$ do *not* include the line.

The following examples show the difference in the solution to the above inequality when the inequality sign is changed.

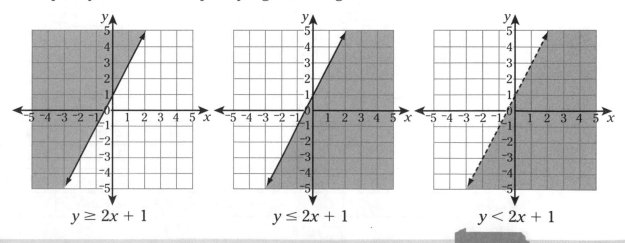

$y \geq 2x + 1$ $y \leq 2x + 1$ $y < 2x + 1$

Unit 4 Linear Inequalities

99

Try this sample question.

S-1 Which inequality is graphed below?

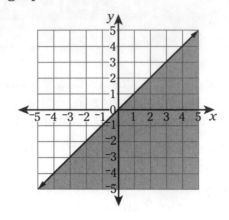

A $y > x$ B $y \geq x$ C $y < x$ D $y \leq x$

In this question, the area below the graph of $y = x$ is shaded. Also, the line itself is solid rather than dashed. Therefore, the graph shown is the graph of $y \leq x$. Choice D is correct.

Systems of Linear Inequalities

Like linear equations, a **system of linear inequalities** can be graphed on the same coordinate plane. The solution to this type of system is the area where their shaded regions overlap.

For example, sketch the graph of the solution to the system of inequalities below.

$$\begin{cases} x + y \geq 2 \\ x - 2y < \text{-}2 \end{cases}$$

First graph the lines $x + y = 2$ and $x - 2y = \text{-}2$. Use a solid line for $x + y = 2$ (because of the $\geq$ sign) and a dotted or dashed line for $x - 2y = \text{-}2$ (because of the $<$ sign).

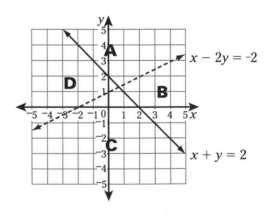

The two lines divide the coordinate plane into four regions, labeled A, B, C, and D as shown here. Now try a test point in each region to find out which region to shade. Find the region where the x- and y-values of the test point satisfy *both* inequalities:

Region	Test Point	$x + y \geq 2$	$x - 2y < \text{-}2$
A	(2, 3)	$2 + 3 \geq 2$: True	$2 - 6 < \text{-}2$: True
B	(4, 1)	$4 + 1 \geq 2$: True	$4 - 2 < \text{-}2$: False
C	(1, 0)	$1 + 0 \geq 2$: False	$1 - 0 < \text{-}2$: False
D	(-2, 2)	$\text{-}2 + 2 \geq 2$: False	$\text{-}2 - 4 < \text{-}2$: True

The test point in region A is the only one that satisfies both inequalities. So region A should be shaded, and the solution looks like this:

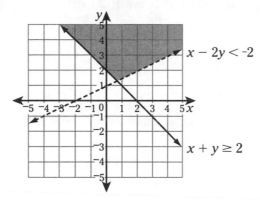

Try this sample question.

S-2 Which graph represents the solution to the system of inequalities shown below?

$$\begin{cases} y \geq 2x - 3 \\ x + y < 4 \end{cases}$$

A

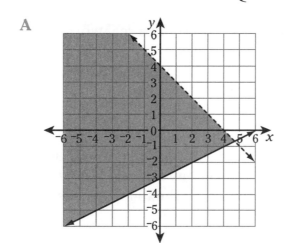

C

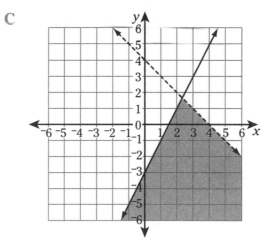

B

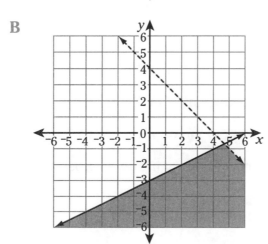

D

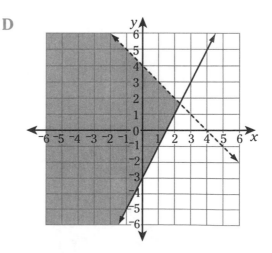

To graph the inequality $y \geq 2x - 3$, first graph $y = 2x - 3$. Test the point $(0, 0)$ to see if this point is included in the solution:

$$y \geq 2x - 3 \rightarrow 0 \geq 2(0) - 3$$

Since $0 \geq -3$, this point is included in the solution. The area to the left of this inequality containing the point $(0, 0)$ should be shaded.

Rewrite the second inequality by solving for y. This will make it easier to graph.

$$x + y < 4 \text{ becomes } y < -x + 4$$

To graph $y < -x + 4$, first graph $y = -x + 4$. The line will be dashed since the inequality does not include the line itself. Test the point $(0, 0)$ to see if this point is included in the solution:

$$y < -x + 4 \rightarrow 0 < 0 + 4$$

Since $0 < 4$, this point is included in the solution. The area below this inequality containing the point $(0, 0)$ should be shaded.

The solution is the area where both shaded regions overlap. Choice D is correct.

Interpreting Solutions to Systems of Inequalities

When a system of inequalities represents a real-world situation, its solution set has specific meaning within the context of the situation. To interpret a solution, solve the system for specific values and decipher the results in light of the given inequality symbols.

Try this sample question.

S-3 Tony has $200 to buy pants and shirts. Pants, x, are $35 a pair, and shirts, y, are $20 each. He will buy no more than 8 items of clothing. This situation can be represented by the following system of inequalities.

$$\begin{cases} x + y \leq 8 \\ 35x + 20y \leq 200 \end{cases}$$

Which of the following is a true statement?

A If Tony buys 2 pairs of pants (x), he can buy up to 6 shirts (y).

B If Tony buys 4 pairs of pants (x), he can buy no more than 4 shirts (y).

C If Tony buys 5 shirts (y), he can buy up to 3 pairs of pants (x).

D If Tony buys 2 shirts (y), he can buy at most 6 pairs of pants (x).

In all four answer choices, the values of *x* and *y* are true for the first inequality, $x + y \leq 8$. To determine if they are true for the second inequality, substitute one of the values into that inequality and solve for the other variable. Be careful to interpret the terms *up to, no more than,* and *at most* correctly. For choice A, substitute 2 for *x:*

$$35(2) + 20y \leq 200$$
$$70 + 20y \leq 200$$
$$20y \leq 130$$
$$y \leq 6.5$$

Keep in mind that pairs of pants and shirts can only be represented by whole numbers, so this answer must be interpreted as less than or equal to 6, in other words, up to 6. In choice B, substituting 4 for *x* results in $y \leq 3$, so this answer is false. In choice C, substituting 5 for *y* results in $x \leq 2.86$ or less than or equal to 2, meaning choice C is not true. In choice D, substituting 2 for *y* results in $x \leq 4.57$ or less than or equal to 4, so choice D is not true. Choice A is correct.

IT'S YOUR TURN

Read the problem. Circle the letter of the best answer.

1. Which graph shows the solution set of the system of inequalities shown below?

$$\begin{cases} y > x + 3 \\ y < {-}x \end{cases}$$

A
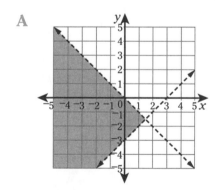

C
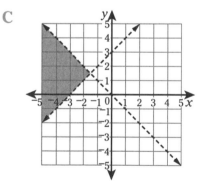

B
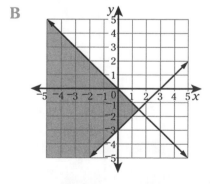

D
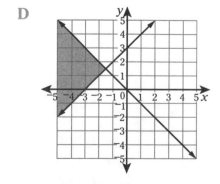

Read each problem. Circle the letter of the best answer.

2. The solution to a system of inequalities is shown below.

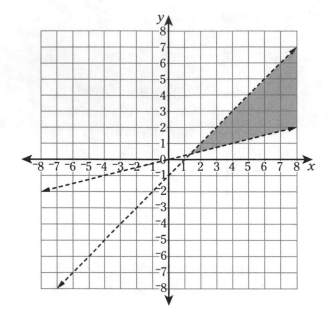

Which system of inequalities does the graph represent?

A $\begin{cases} y < x - 1 \\ y < \frac{1}{4}x \end{cases}$

B $\begin{cases} y > x - 1 \\ y > \frac{1}{4}x \end{cases}$

C $\begin{cases} y > x - 1 \\ y < \frac{1}{4}x \end{cases}$

D $\begin{cases} y < x - 1 \\ y > \frac{1}{4}x \end{cases}$

3. Lorenzo has 46-cent stamps and 20-cent stamps. He needs to use stamps totaling at least $3.00 to mail a package. There is enough room for up to 9 stamps on the package. This situation can be represented by the following system of inequalities, where x = number of 46-cent stamps and y = number of 20-cent stamps.

$$\begin{cases} x + y \leq 9 \\ 46x + 20y \geq 300 \end{cases}$$

Which of the following is a true statement?

A Lorenzo can use four 46-cent stamps and six 20-cent stamps.

B Lorenzo can use five 46-cent stamps and four 20-cent stamps.

C If Lorenzo uses six 46-cent stamps, he only needs to use one 20-cent stamp.

D If Lorenzo uses twelve 20-cent stamps, he only needs to use one 46-cent stamp.

Read each problem. Circle the letter of the best answer.

4. Which of the following graphs represents the solution to the system of inequalities given below?

$$\begin{cases} y < x - 3 \\ y \geq -\dfrac{1}{2}x \end{cases}$$

A
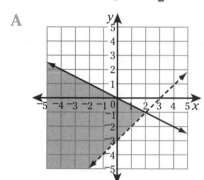

B
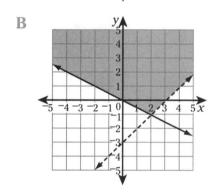

C
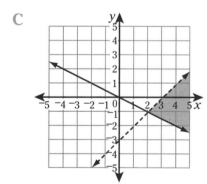

D
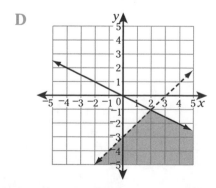

5. Jina is raising money for a charity. She makes either 18 telephone calls per day or 10 home visits per day. Jina wants to contact at least 100 people next week. This situation can be represented by the following system of inequalities, where x = number of days making telephone calls and y = number of days making home visits.

$$\begin{cases} x + y \leq 7 \\ 18x + 10y \geq 100 \end{cases}$$

Which of the following is a true statement?

A Jina can reach her goal by making home visits only.

B Jina can reach her goal with only 2 days of telephone calls.

C If Jina does home visits for 4 days, she only needs 2 days of telephone calls.

D If Jina makes telephone calls for 5 days, she only needs 1 day of home visits.

Read each problem. Circle the letter of the best answer.

6. Which system of inequalities is shown?

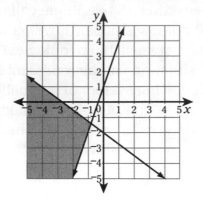

A $\begin{cases} 3x - y \le -1 \\ 3x + 4y \le -8 \end{cases}$

B $\begin{cases} 3x - y \le -1 \\ 3x + 4y \ge -8 \end{cases}$

C $\begin{cases} 3x - y \ge -1 \\ 3x + 4y \le -8 \end{cases}$

D $\begin{cases} 3x - y \ge -1 \\ 3x + 4y \ge -8 \end{cases}$

7. At an ice-cream parlor, ice-cream cones cost x dollars each and sundaes cost y dollars each. The total cost of 4 cones and 3 sundaes is more than $20. The total cost of 5 cones and 1 sundae is less than $16. This situation can be represented by the following system of inequalities.

$$\begin{cases} 4x + 3y > 20 \\ 5x + y < 16 \end{cases}$$

Which of the following is **not** possible?

A The cost of 1 sundae is $4.00.

B The cost of 1 ice-cream cone is $2.50.

C The total cost of 1 ice-cream cone and 1 sundae is $5.00.

D The total cost of 1 ice-cream cone and 1 sundae is $8.00.

8. Which system of inequalities is modeled by the graph below?

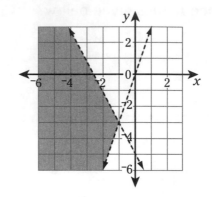

A $\begin{cases} y > 3x \\ y < -2x - 5 \end{cases}$

B $\begin{cases} y < 3x \\ y < -2x - 5 \end{cases}$

C $\begin{cases} y > 3x \\ y > -2x - 5 \end{cases}$

D $\begin{cases} y < 3x \\ y > -2x - 5 \end{cases}$

9. Which graph shows the solution to the system of inequalities shown below?

$$\begin{cases} y < x + 4 \\ y \geq 2x \end{cases}$$

A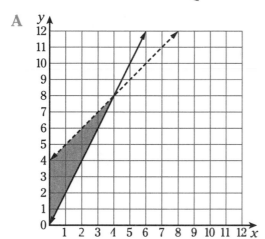

C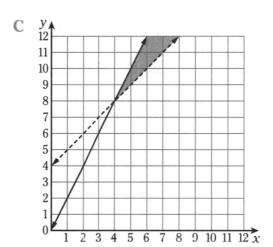

B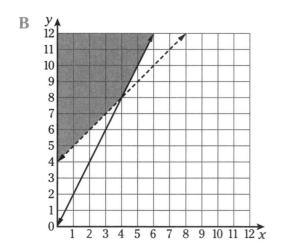

D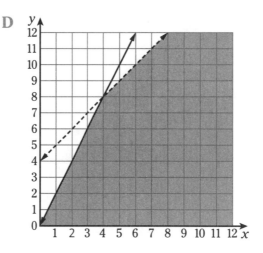

Read the problem. Write your answer for each part.

1. Two inequalities are shown below.

$$-26 < 4k - 2 \qquad 2k - 1 < 5$$

A Write a compound inequality to combine the inequalities above.

Answer: _____

B Solve your compound inequality for values of k. Show your work.

Answer: _____

C Graph your solution on the number line below.

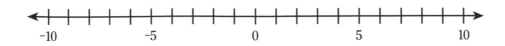

Read the problem. Write your answer for each part.

2. Paul is going to solve the inequality shown below. In the inequality, w represents the width of a rectangle.

$$|4 - 3w| \geq 8$$

A Solve the inequality. Show your work.

Answer: _____

B Graph the solution to the inequality on this number line.

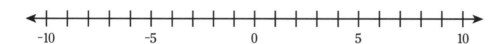

C Paul says that $w = -3$ is a reasonable solution to the inequality. Explain why Paul thinks that, but also explain why he is incorrect in this situation.

Read the problem. Write your answer for each part.

3. The annual expenses of a non-profit organization must satisfy the inequality below, where x = millions of dollars.

$$2(x - 5) \geq 6(x - 3)$$

A Graph the solution set to this inequality on the number line below.

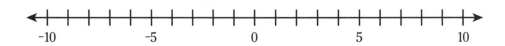

B The annual contributions that the organization hopes to collect next year are represented by the inequality that is graphed below, where x = millions of dollars.

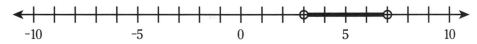

The inequality has the form $7 <$ _____ < 15. What expression belongs on the blank line so that the inequality has the solution graphed above?

Answer: _____

C The solution set to a system of linear inequalities is graphed
below.

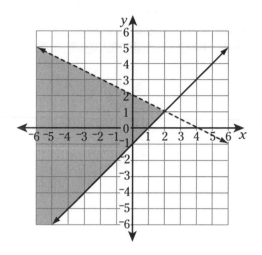

Write a system of two linear inequalities that would have the
solution set shown in the graph.

Answer: _____

Read the problem. Write your answer for each part.

4. Michele is a photographer. She sells framed photographs for $100 each and greeting cards for $5 each. The materials for each framed photograph cost $30, and the materials for each greeting card cost $2. Michele can sell up to 8 framed photographs and 40 greeting cards each week, but this week she has only $200 to spend on materials. Michele hopes to earn a profit of at least $400 this week after paying for materials.

Let x = the number of framed photographs and y = the number of greeting cards Michele will make and sell this week. Two of the inequalities that model this situation are $x \le 8$ and $y \le 40$.

A Write two more inequalities to complete the system of inequalities modeling the situation.

Answers: _____ and _____

B Graph the solution set to your system of inequalities on this coordinate plane. Shade the area that represents the solution set.

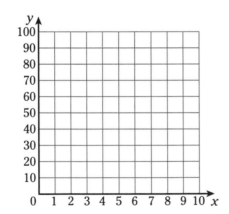

C Michele plans to make and sell 5 framed photographs and 25 greeting cards. Is that a solution to the system of inequalities? If so, is it the solution that will produce the **most** profit? Explain your answers.

Read the problem. Write your answer for each part.

5. A band sells CDs for $8 each and T-shirts for $15 each. Sarah wants to buy some CDs and T-shirts as gifts for her friends, but she can spend a total of $75 at most.

  A Write an inequality using *x* and *y* variables to represent this situation.

    Answer: _____

  B Explain what the variables *x* and *y* represent in your inequality.

  C Graph your inequality on this coordinate plane. Shade the area that represents the solution set.

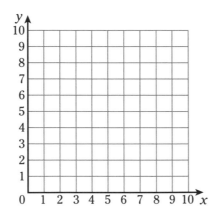

  D Provide two different solutions to your inequality.

    Answer: _____ and _____

Module 2
Linear Functions and Data Organizations

Unit 5
Functions

Identifying and Representing Patterns

A1.2.1.1.1

Patterns

Much of mathematics is concerned with identifying a **pattern,** or sequence. An **arithmetic pattern** is a sequence of numbers that changes by adding or subtracting the same value from one term to the next. The key to recognizing and describing an arithmetic pattern is to look for a common sum or difference from one term of the pattern to the next.

For example, consider the sequence 9, 16, 23, 30, 37, ….

$$16 - 9 = 7$$
$$23 - 16 = 7$$
$$30 - 23 = 7$$
$$37 - 30 = 7$$

This sequence forms an arithmetic pattern. The difference between one term and the next is always 7, a constant. So to continue this sequence, keep adding 7.

Try this sample question.

S-1 Look at the pattern below.

$$48, 39, 30, 21, …$$

If the pattern continues, what will be the seventh term?

A -6   **B** 3   **C** 12   **D** 15

The difference between 48 and 39 is 9. And the difference between 39 and 30 is 9. Therefore, starting at 48, you subtract 9 from each term to get the next one. The fourth term is 21, so the fifth term is $21 - 9 = 12$. The sixth is $12 - 9 = 3$, and the seventh is $3 - 9 = $ -6. So the seventh term in the pattern is -6. Choice A is correct.

Describing Patterns Algebraically

Many number patterns can be expressed using algebraic symbols. Look again at the sequence shown in the section above: 9, 16, 23, 30, 37…. To describe this sequence using algebra, let the variable n represent any given term number in the sequence. The number being added to each term is 7. The first term, 9, is 2 more than this common number. So, the expression $7n + 2$ can be used to find any given term in the sequence.

Unit 5 Functions

Try this sample question.

S-2 The first term in the pattern below is 6.

$$6, 1, -4, -9, -14, \ldots$$

Which expression can be used to find the nth term in this pattern?

  A $n - 5$ **B** $-5n + 6$ **C** $-5n + 11$ **D** $-6n + 5$

The difference between any two consecutive terms is -5. The first term in the pattern is 11 more than this common difference. So the expression $-5n + 11$ can be used to find any term, n, in this pattern. You can check this by substituting term numbers for n to see if the correct term value results. When $n = 2$, $-5n + 11 = -5(2) + 11 = 1$. The number 1 is the second term in the pattern. When $n = 3$, $-5n + 11 = -5(3) + 11 = -4$. The number -4 is the third term in the pattern. This is also true for the other given terms in the pattern. Choice C is correct.

Representing Patterns Graphically

Sometimes a pattern will be presented verbally, in a word problem. The pattern from the word problem can then be represented in a graph.

For example, suppose that a park ranger counts 60 turtles living in a lake and expects the turtle population to increase by 10 turtles per year. Then the predicted turtle population will form the pattern 60, 70, 80, 90, …. This is a pattern you could describe in words ("each term is 10 greater than the previous term") or as an algebraic expression. If you let t be the number of years after the turtles were originally counted, then the expression $10t + 60$ describes this pattern. Number patterns can also be described using a graph. The graph shown here describes this pattern.

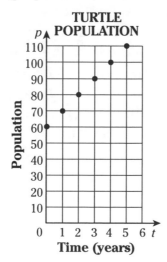

Try this sample question.

S-3 Kerim bought a $2,000 bicycle. The bicycle's value depreciates, or decreases, by $300 a year. Which graph represents this situation?

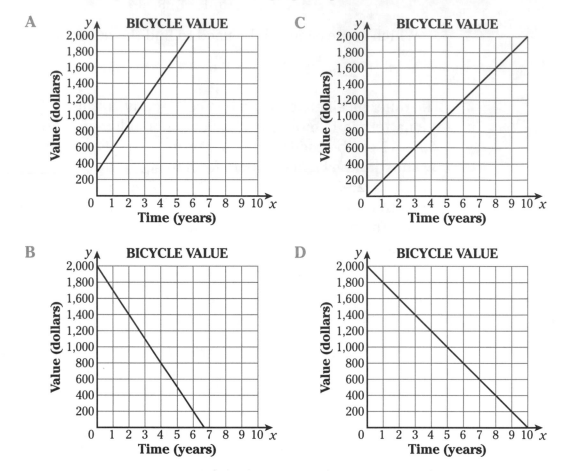

The value of the bicycle drops by $300 a year, so a line representing its value would slant downward from left to right. Choices A and C show increasing values, so they are not correct. Choices B and D both show decreasing values that start from $2,000, the bicycle's value when purchased, or at 0 years. After 1 year, the value will be $2,000 − $300 = $1,700. Check the points representing the value after one year on each graph: in choice D, the coordinates for this point are (1, 1,800); in choice B, the coordinates are (1, 1,700). Choice B is correct.

Read each problem. Circle the letter of the best answer.

1. Look at the pattern below.

   8, 17, 26, 35, 44, …

   Which expression represents this pattern algebraically?

   A $n + 9$

   B $n - 9$

   C $9n + 1$

   D $9n - 1$

2. In a chemistry experiment, the temperature of a gas, in degrees Celsius, followed this pattern.

   TEMPERATURE OF GAS

Number of Seconds After Reaction (t)	Temperature of Gas (°C)
0	300
1	285
2	270
3	255

   Which of these expressions describes the pattern?

   A $300 - 15t$

   B $300 + 15t$

   C $300t - 15$

   D $300t + 15$

3. The expression $12x + 6$ can be used to describe a sequence algebraically. Which of the following could be the first five numbers in this sequence?

   A 6, 12, 18, 24, 30

   B 6, 18, 24, 36, 42

   C 18, 30, 42, 54, 66

   D 18, 36, 54, 72, 90

4. The Fisher family sells quilts over the Internet. The graph below shows the relationship between the number of quilts they sell and the amount of money they receive.

   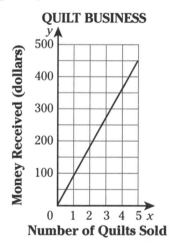

   QUILT BUSINESS

   Which of these equations shows the same information as the graph, where N is the number of quilts sold and M is the amount of money, in dollars?

   A $M = 90 \cdot N$

   B $M = 90 + N$

   C $M = 90 - N$

   D $M = 90 \div N$

Read each problem. Circle the letter of the best answer.

5. The data below shows a Chihuahua puppy's weight, in ounces, on the day it was born and on the next five days.

   3.75, 4.25, 4.75, 5.25, 5.75, 6.25

   Which graph shows this data?

   A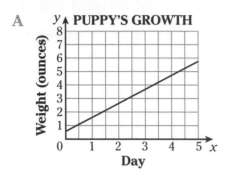

   B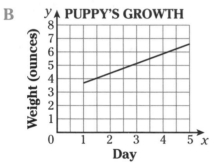

   C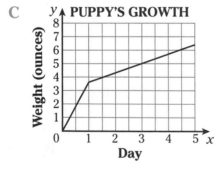

   D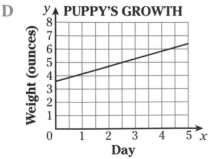

6. Holly shipped a 5-pound package for $4. She shipped a 3-pound package for $3.60 and a 1-pound package for $3.20. A 10-pound package cost $5 to ship. The cost follows a pattern based on the weight. Which expression could be used to find the shipping cost for a package of p pounds?

   A $0.2p + 3$

   B $2p + 3$

   C $0.3p + 2$

   D $3p + 2$

7. The table shows how the amount remaining to pay on an automobile loan is changing over time.

   AUTO LOAN PAYOFF

Time (months)	Amount Remaining (dollars)
0	5,000
1	4,800
2	4,600
3	4,400
4	4,200

   Let x represent the time in months, and let y represent the amount in dollars remaining to pay. Which equation describes the relationship between x and y?

   A $y = -800x + 5,000$

   B $y = -200x + 5,000$

   C $y = 200x - 5,000$

   D $y = 800x - 5,000$

Relations and Functions

A1.2.1.1.2, A1.2.1.1.3

A **relation** is a set of ordered pairs (input, output). These ordered pairs are often written within braces. For example, the ordered pairs for (age, height) shown below form a relation.

$$\{(15, 65), (21, 70), (18, 73), (16, 62)\}$$

Identifying Domain and Range

The **domain** of a relation is the set of all input values. The **range** is the set of all output values. The domain of the relation above is {15, 21, 18, 16}. Its range is {65, 70, 73, 62}.

In ordered pairs (x, y), the x-values are the domain and the y-values are the range.

Try this sample question.

S-1 The number of laps some students ran around the school track and the number of minutes they ran are shown in the table below.

Laps	3	8	5	6	4
Minutes	9	14	9	15	8

What is the range of this relation?

A {3, 4, 5, 6, 8}

B {8, 9, 14, 15}

C {3, 4, 5, 6, 14, 15}

D {3, 4, 5, 6, 8, 9, 14, 15}

The range is the set of output values. In the table, laps are the input and minutes are the output. So the range is the set containing the number of minutes {8, 9, 14, 15}. Repeated numbers are written once. Choice B is correct.

Identifying Functions from Relations

A relation that assigns a unique range value for every domain value is called a **function.** With ordered pairs in the form (x, y), the x-values are the domain and the y-values are the range. You can determine if a relation is a function using any of these methods:

• Check that no domain values are repeated.

• Analyze the graph of a relation.

• Use a mapping diagram.

A function assigns each x-value to one and only one y-value.

A **vertical-line test** can be used on a graph to determine if a relation is a function. If a vertical line passes through no more than one point at a time on the graph, the relation is a function. For example, look at the two graphs below.

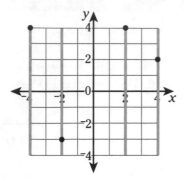

This graph is a function since each vertical line drawn passes through only one point. Each domain value (x) has only one range value (y).

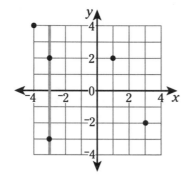

This graph is *not* a function since a vertical line passes through more than one point. The domain value -3 has two range values, 2 and -3.

Some relations are graphed as a set of continuous points that form a straight or curved line or part of a line. For example, in the graph below, data is continuous at all x-values from -5 to 5 except for at $x = 3$, where there is a break in the graph.

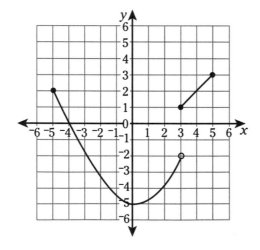

Notice the open circle at (3, -2), and the closed circle at (3, 1). The open circle means the point (3, -2) is *not* part of the graph. The closed circle means the point (3, 1) *is* part of the graph. Having one open and one closed circle at points when $x = 3$ means that x-value corresponds to only one y-value. Therefore, this relation is a function. The vertical line test can also be used to show this.

Try this sample question.

S-2 Which statement best describes the relation graphed below?

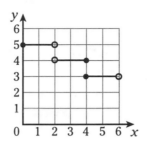

A The relation is a function since the *x*-value 2 does not correspond to any *y*-value.

B The relation is not a function since the *x*-value 4 corresponds to more than one *y*-value.

C The relation is a function since the *x*-values from 0 to 6 correspond to only one *y*-value each.

D The relation is not a function since the *y*-values 3, 4, and 5 correspond to more than one *x*-value.

In order for a relation to be a function, each *x*-value must correspond to no more than one *y*-value. The *x*-values in this graph include all numbers from 0 to 6, except for 2 and 6. The closed circles mean those points are part of the graph. The open circles mean those points are not part of the graph. In choice A, it is true that the *x*-value 2 corresponds to no *y*-value. But this only means the relation is not continuous. Since there are two closed circles at $x = 4$, this *x*-value corresponds to two *y*-values, 3 and 4. For that reason, this relation is not a function. You can also see that this graph does not pass the vertical line test at $x = 4$. Choice B is correct.

A **mapping** is another way of determining if a relation is a function. In a mapping, arrows are typically drawn from the domain of a relation to its range. If no more than one arrow is drawn from any domain value to a range value, the relation is a function. Otherwise, it is not. Here are two examples.

Relation A

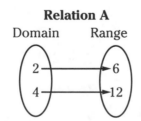

Relation A is a function.

Relation B

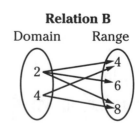

Relation B is not a function.

Try this sample question.

S-3 Which relation is also a function?

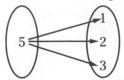

A Domain   Range

C Domain   Range

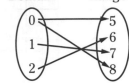

B Domain   Range

D Domain   Range

The arrows in these mappings show the domain values that correspond to the range values. In a function, each domain value corresponds to only one range value. So, the mapping that is a function has exactly one arrow from each domain value to any range value. Choices A, B, and D show at least two arrows pointing from the same domain value. Only choice C shows one arrow pointing from each domain value. Choice C is correct.

IT'S YOUR TURN

Read each problem. Circle the letter of the best answer.

1. The number of hours the waitstaff at Emilio's Restaurant worked one day and the amount in tips each person got is shown in the table below.

Hours Worked	4	6	5	2
$ in Tips	40	45	36	16

What is the range of this relation?

A {2, 4, 5, 6}

B {2, 4, 5, 6, 16}

C {16, 36, 40, 45}

D {2, 4, 5, 6, 16, 26, 40, 45}

2. What is the domain of the relation graphed below?

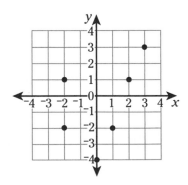

A {-2, 1, 2, 3}

B {-4, -2, 1, 3}

C {-2, 0, 1, 2, 3}

D {-2, -1, 0, 1, 2, 3}

Read each problem. Circle the letter of the best answer.

3. Which relation is also a function?

   A {(0, 3), (4, 3), (8, 3)}

   B {(1, 2), (2, 3), (1, 4)}

   C {(4, 5), (4, 7), (4, 9)}

   D {(6, 0), (8, 1), (8, 5)}

4. Which table of values represents a function?

   A

x	y
8	-2
0	-1
-1	5
8	-9

   B

x	y
-2	3
0	-3
-2	8
6	-1

   C

x	y
5	0
5	3
5	-7
5	-9

   D

x	y
7	-2
-3	-2
9	-2
-4	-2

5. Which graph represents a function?

   A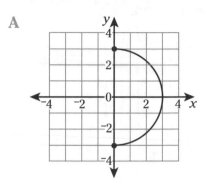

   B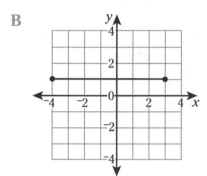

   C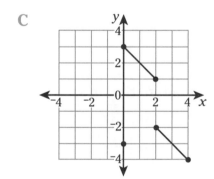

   D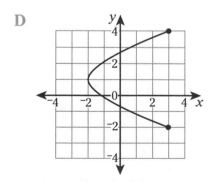

Read each problem. Circle the letter of the best answer.

6. The coordinate plane below shows the graph of a relation.

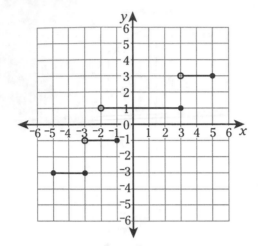

What is the range of the graph?

A $-3 \leq y \leq 3$

B $-5 \leq x \leq 5$

C $\{-3, -1, 1, 3\}$

D $\{-3, 3\}$

7. The graph of a function is shown below.

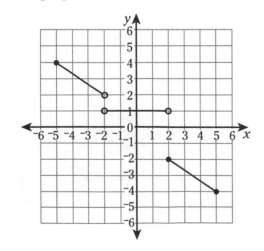

Which value is **not** in the domain of the function?

A -2   C 0

B -1   D 2

8. Which relation is also a function?

A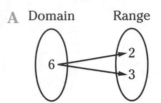

B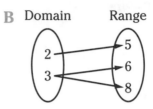

C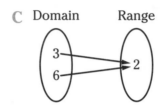

D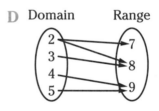

9. Look at this set of ordered pairs.

{(2, 4), (3, 4), (4, 6), (5, 6), (6, 8), (7, 8)}

Which statement about the relation above is true?

A It is a function because every *x*-value is unique.

B It is a function because every *x*-value has only one *y*-value.

C It is not a function because the *y*-values repeat.

D It is not a function because every *y*-value has more than one *x*-value.

Linear Functions

A1.2.1.2.1, A1.2.1.2.2

Linear functions can be represented using equations, tables, and graphs. Being able to identify different representations of the same function is a valuable skill to have. You should also be able to translate a real-life situation described in words into an equation, a table, or a graph, and to interpret the meaning of the linear function.

> A **linear function** is a function whose graph is a straight line.

Finding Graphs of Linear Functions

One way to connect a function with its equation is to find some points that make the equation true. Then plot these ordered pairs on a coordinate plane. For example, to find the graph for the equation $y = -x - 1$, first find points to make the equation true: $(0, -1)$, $(1, -2)$, $(2, -3)$, $(-1, 0)$, $(-2, 1)$. Then plot these points. The graph of this linear function is shown here.

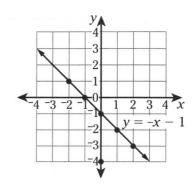

Try this sample question.

S-1 A company estimates its total monthly expenses using the equation $y = 4,000x + 4,000$. Which of these graphs shows this relationship?

A

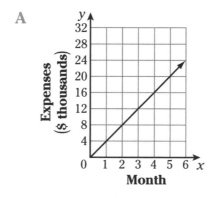

C

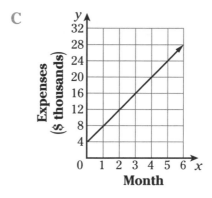

B

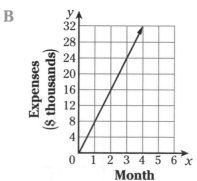

D

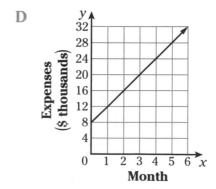

First choose some values for x and solve the equation for y. You can make a table to keep track of your pairs.

Month	1	2	3	4
Expenses ($)	8,000	12,000	16,000	20,000

Rewrite the points shown in your table as the set of ordered pairs (1, 8,000), (2, 12,000), (3, 16,000), and (4, 20,000). Look at each graph. Find the graph that contains these ordered pairs. Only the graph in choice C contains all of these points. Choice C is correct.

Finding Tables of Linear Functions

Sometimes a linear function is described verbally. Translating the words into mathematical expressions and creating a table of values can help you recognize the function.

Consider this example: Shaya is selling sandwiches for a fundraiser. The sandwiches cost $6 each. There is a delivery charge of $2 per order. The input values for a representative table would be n, the number of sandwiches in an order. The output values would be the cost, c, of the order, $6n + 2$. An order of 1 sandwich would be $6 \cdot 1 + 2 = 8$. An order of 2 sandwiches would be $6 \cdot 2 + 2 = 14$, and so on. A table of values representing this function is shown here.

Number of Sandwiches (n)	Total Cost (c)
1	8
2	14
3	20
4	26

Try this sample question.

S-2 Ethan could do only 5 crunches before he began a training program. At the end of each day of training, he was able to do 2 more crunches than the day before. Which table shows how many crunches Ethan could do after 0, 5, 10, and 15 days of training?

A

Day (d)	Number of Crunches (c)
0	5
5	10
10	20
15	30

C

Day (d)	Number of Crunches (c)
0	7
5	17
10	27
15	37

B

Day (d)	Number of Crunches (c)
0	5
5	15
10	25
15	35

D

Day (d)	Number of Crunches (c)
0	5
5	27
10	52
15	77

The phrase *before training* can be interpreted as day 0. Since Ethan could do 5 crunches then, the values for this point are $(0, 5)$. On each day of training, d, the number of crunches increases by 2, so the increase can be represented as $2d$. This number is in addition to the initial 5 crunches, so the output value is $2d + 5$. Substitute the values 0, 5, 10, and 15 into this expression to find c, the number of crunches he could do: $2 \cdot 0 + 5 = 5$, $2 \cdot 5 + 5 = 15$, $2 \cdot 10 + 5 = 25$, $2 \cdot 15 + 5 = 35$. Then locate the table with 5, 15, 25, and 35 for the output values. Choice B is correct.

Interpreting Linear Functions

Whether presented as an equation, a table of values, or a graph, a linear function for a real-life-situation has a specific meaning within the context of the situation. Correctly interpreting the form is crucial to understanding the function.

Try this sample question.

S-3　An online booking agency charges for tickets and includes a ticketing fee for each order. The total charge, c, in dollars, for any number of tickets, t, is described by the function $c = 20t + 4$. Which statement is true?

　A　The cost of 20 tickets is $80.

　B　The cost of 4 tickets is $20.

　C　Each ticket costs $20, and the ticketing fee is $4.

　D　Each ticket costs $4, and the ticketing fee is $20.

Consider the meanings of the variables: c is total cost, a dollar value, and t is a quantity, a number of tickets. Since a number t times something results in a dollar amount, 20 must be a dollar amount, the price per ticket. The ticketing fee is also a dollar amount, but it is a constant separate from the individual ticket cost. So $4 is the ticketing fee. Choice C is correct.

Read each problem. Circle the letter of the best answer.

1. Which graph models the equation $2x + 3y = -6$?

A

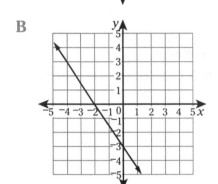

B

C

D

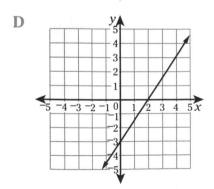

2. The graph shows how the amount of grain in storage in a certain country is changing over time.

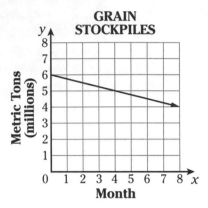

Which equation describes the linear function graphed above?

A $y = -4x + 6$

B $y = -\frac{1}{4}x + 6$

C $y = \frac{1}{4}x + 6$

D $y = 4x + 6$

3. Jazmin is a hairdresser who rents a station in a salon for a daily fee. The amount of money (m) Jazmin makes from any number of haircuts (n) a day is described by the linear function $m = 45n - 30$. Which statement is true?

A A haircut costs $30, and the station rent is $45.

B A haircut costs $45, and the station rent is $30.

C Jazmin must do 30 haircuts to pay the $45 rental fee.

D Jazmin deducts $30 from each $45 haircut for the station rent.

Read each problem. Circle the letter of the best answer.

4. Yolanda saves all the money from a regular baby-sitting job. The money in her savings account is increasing according to the linear equation $y = 6x + 50$, where $x =$ number of hours worked and $y =$ savings in dollars. Which table of values matches this equation?

A

x	y
0	0
5	80
10	160
15	240

B

x	y
0	0
5	30
10	60
15	90

C

x	y
0	50
5	100
10	150
15	200

D

x	y
0	50
5	80
10	110
15	140

5. The table below shows the number of defective batteries identified in different shipments.

BATTERY INSPECTION

Batteries in Shipment (n)	Defective Batteries (d)
100	2
200	4
300	6
400	8
500	10

Which linear equation shows the relationship between the total number of batteries in the shipment and the number of defective batteries?

A $d = 100n$

B $d = 50n$

C $d = 0.01n$

D $d = 0.02n$

Read each problem. Circle the letter of the best answer.

6. A jet is traveling at 800 kilometers per hour. Which graph best shows the relationship between time and distance traveled for this jet?

A
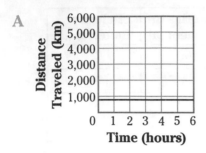

B
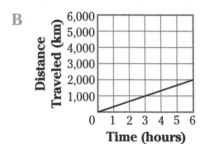

C
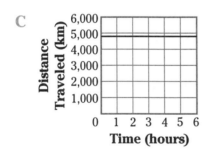

D
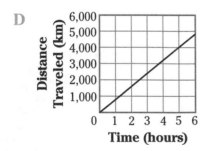

7. Quentin is filling a bicycle tire with air. The air pressure started at 20 pounds per square inch (psi), and is increasing by 1.5 psi per second. Which table shows the relationship between time and air pressure?

A
Time (seconds)	Air Pressure (psi)
0	21.5
2	24.5
4	27.5
6	30.5
8	33.5

B
Time (seconds)	Air Pressure (psi)
0	20
2	21.5
4	23
6	24.5
8	26

C
Time (seconds)	Air Pressure (psi)
0	20
2	22
4	24
6	26
8	28

D
Time (seconds)	Air Pressure (psi)
0	20
2	23
4	26
6	29
8	32

Read each problem. Circle the letter of the best answer.

8. The graph below shows how the monthly rent for an apartment changed over time.

Which statement about the linear function shown by the graph is true?

A Every year the rent goes up $600.

B Every year the rent is $50 more than the first year.

C Every year the rent is $50 more than the previous year.

D Every year the rent is $100 more than the previous year.

9. The Garcia family drives home from a vacation trip. The table of values below shows the relationship between the number of gallons, g, of gasoline their car uses and the distance in miles, d, the car is from home.

Gallons of Gasoline Used (g)	Distance from Home (d)
1	144
2	124
3	104
4	84
5	64

Which statement is true?

A The Garcias drove 144 miles on 5 gallons of gas to get home.

B The Garcias drove a total of 144 miles in 5 hours to get home.

C The Garcias were 144 miles away when they started home and their car got 20 miles to the gallon.

D The Garcias were 164 miles away when they started home and their car got 20 miles to the gallon.

Read the problem. Circle the letter of the best answer.

10. The table shows how the temperature of the water in a lake depends on depth.

LAKE WATER TEMPERATURE

Depth (meters)	Temperature (°C)
0	8.0
1	7.2
2	6.4
3	5.6
4	4.8
5	4.0

Which graph shows this relationship?

A

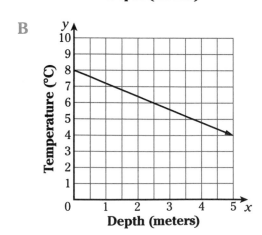

C

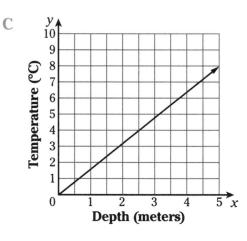

B

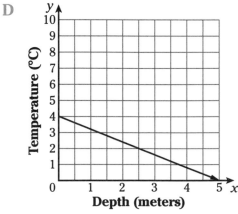

D

Read the problem. Write your answer for each part.

1. During the summer, Kaleighna mows lawns to earn money. She keeps track of the number of lawns she mows and how many hours it takes her each day for five days. The table below shows her data for one week.

Number of Lawns	4	2	2	3	1
Number of Hours	3	5	2	5	1

   A Graph the points from the table above. Label each axis.

   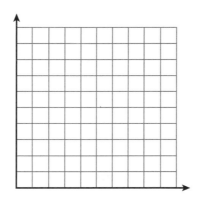

   B Identify the domain and range of the data. Name the values and what they represent.

   Domain: _____

   Range: _____

   C Explain how you know whether or not this relation is a function.

Read the problem. Write your answer for each part.

2. Justin works at a shop that prints T-shirts. The table shows how the cost of printing T-shirts depends on the number printed.

T-SHIRT PRINTING COSTS

Number of T-Shirts	Total Cost (dollars)
20	110
30	135
40	160
50	185
60	210

A Write an equation to show the relationship between *n*, the number of T-shirts printed, and *C*, the total cost in dollars.

Answer: _____

B Graph your equation on this coordinate plane. Be sure to include an appropriate scale on each axis.

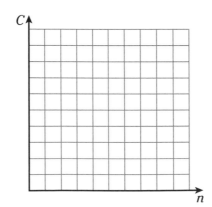

C What would be the total cost of an order of 120 T-shirts?

Answer: _____

D Explain how you found your answer to **part C.**

Read the problem. Write your answer for each part.

3. The graph shows how the length of a building's shadow at a certain time of day is related to the height of the building.

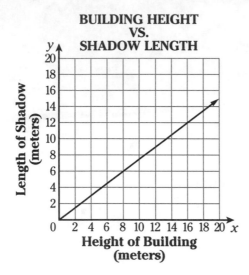

BUILDING HEIGHT VS. SHADOW LENGTH

A Does this graph describe a function? Explain why or why not.

B Write an equation to describe the relationship shown in the graph.

Answer: _____

C Explain the meaning of the variables in your equation.

D According to your equation, if a building is 160 meters tall, what would be the length of its shadow?

Answer: _____

Read the problem. Write your answer for each part.

4. During the fall in the Northern Hemisphere, the amount of daylight decreases each day. On September 21st in a certain town, the daylight was changing according to the equation $y = -0.05x + 12$, where x = time in days and y = daylight length in hours.

   A Graph the function $y = -0.05x + 12$ for $-40 \leq x \leq 40$ on this coordinate plane.

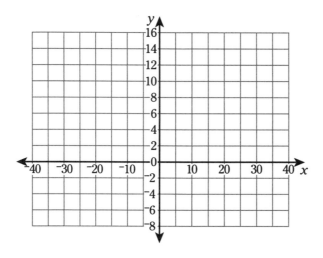

   B What are the domain and range of the part of the function you graphed?

      Answer: _____

C What is the meaning of the point on your graph where $x = -40$? Explain.

D Explain why the function $y = -0.05x + 12$ **cannot** describe the changing amount of daylight for an entire year.

Read the problem. Write your answer for each part.

5. Olivia bought a houseplant that was 8 inches tall. It began growing taller at a rate of 2 inches every 3 months.

   A Let h represent the plant's height in inches t months after Olivia bought it. Complete the table below to show the values of h for $t = 0, 3, 6, 9,$ and 12.

t	h

   B Write an equation that describes the relationship between t and h.

Answer: _____

   C Use your equation to find how many months it will take the plant to reach a height of 21 inches. Show your work.

Answer: _____

Module 2
Linear Functions and Data Organizations

Unit 6
Coordinate Geometry

Slope, Intercepts, and Rates of Change

A1.2.2.1.1, A1.2.2.1.2, A1.2.2.1.4

Slope

Slope is a measure of the steepness of a line. It describes a rate of change. The slope of a line can be found using either of these methods:

1. On the graph of a line, determine the vertical change (the "rise") over the horizontal change (the "run") from one point to another.

$$\text{slope} = \frac{\text{vertical change}}{\text{horizontal change}} = \frac{\text{``rise''}}{\text{``run''}}$$

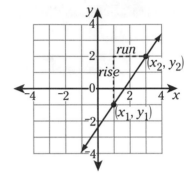

2. Use the **slope formula.** For any two points on a line, (x_1, y_1) and (x_2, y_2) and $x_1 \neq x_2$,

$$\text{slope} = \frac{y_2 - y_1}{x_2 - x_1}.$$

A line that slants upward from left to right always has a positive slope. A line that slants downward from left to right always has a negative slope.

It is a good idea to check the slope of a line found when looking at a graph using rise over run by also using the slope formula.

> Horizontal lines have a slope of 0.
> Vertical lines have an undefined slope.

Try this sample question.

S-1 What is the slope of the line graphed below?

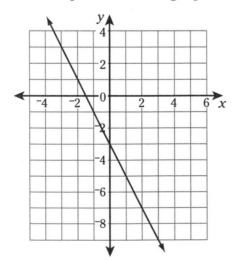

A −3   B −2   C $-\dfrac{1}{2}$ D $-\dfrac{1}{3}$

Unit 6 Coordinate Geometry

Find the slope using the rise over the run, or $\frac{rise}{run}$. By looking at the graph, you can see that the line has a rise of -2 and a run of 1, so the slope is $\frac{-2}{1}$ or -2. Verify this slope by using the slope formula with any two points on the graph.

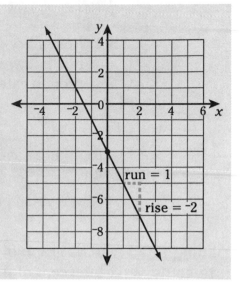

$$\text{Slope} = \frac{-5 - (-3)}{1 - 0} = \frac{-5 + 3}{1} = \frac{-2}{1} \text{ or } -2.$$

Both methods result in the same slope. Choice B is correct.

Rates of Change and Applications of Slope

A **rate of change** shows the relationship between two quantities that are changing. This change can be constant or it can vary. The rate of change of a linear function is constant and the same as the slope of the function.

Slope can be used to find different rates of change, such as the grade of a road or the pitch of a roof. The greater the slope, the steeper the road or the roof pitch. For example, suppose an architect draws the two roofs shown on the coordinate planes below.

Roof A

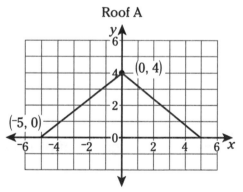

Roof B

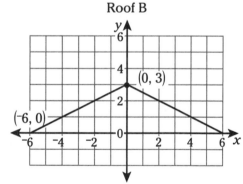

The coordinates of the left side of each roof drawing are shown. Use these coordinates and the slope formula to find the slope of each roof.

The slope of roof A is $\frac{4 - 0}{0 - (-5)} = \frac{4}{5}$. The slope of roof B is $\frac{3 - 0}{0 - (-6)} = \frac{3}{6} = \frac{1}{2}$. The slope of roof A is greater than the slope of roof B since $\frac{4}{5} > \frac{1}{2}$. So roof A is steeper than roof B.

> For any two points on a line (x_1, y_1) and (x_2, y_2) and $x_1 \neq x_2$, the slope of the line is $\frac{y_2 - y_1}{x_2 - x_1}$.

Try this sample question.

S-2 Rosemary grows a plant from seed. In 2 weeks, the plant is 5 centimeters tall. In 6 weeks, the plant is 17 centimeters tall. What is the average growth rate each week of this plant between weeks 2 and 6?

A 3 cm   B 4 cm   C 8 cm   D 12 cm

To find the average growth rate each week, find the slope of the line between the points $(2, 5)$ and $(6, 17)$. Slope $m = \dfrac{y_2 - y_1}{x_2 - x_1} = \dfrac{17 - 5}{6 - 2} = \dfrac{12}{4} = 3$. Choice A is correct.

Finding Intercepts from Graphs

On the graph of a line, the point where the line touches the x-axis is the **x-intercept** of the line. The point where the line touches the y-axis is the **y-intercept** of the line.

For example, on the graph below, the line touches the x-axis at $x = 4$ and the y-axis at $y = -2$. The x-intercept of this line is the point $(4, 0)$. The y-intercept is the point $(0, -2)$.

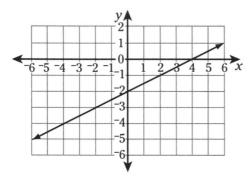

If a line touches the x-axis at $x = a$, the x-intercept is the point $(a, 0)$.
If a line touches the y-axis at $y = b$, the y-intercept is the point $(0, b)$.

Try this sample question.

S-3 Which statement best describes the graph of the line shown below?

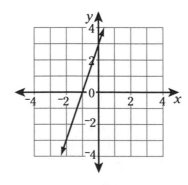

A The slope is positive and the x-intercept is -1.

B The slope is negative and the x-intercept is 3.

C The slope is positive and the y-intercept is -1.

D The slope is negative and the y-intercept is 3.

Unit 6 Coordinate Geometry

The line on the graph slants upward from left to right, so the slope is positive. The line touches the x-axis at -1 and it touches the y-axis at 3. So the x-intercept is -1 and the y-intercept is 3. Choice A is correct.

IT'S YOUR TURN

Read each problem. Circle the letter of the best answer.

1. A linear equation is graphed on the coordinate plane below.

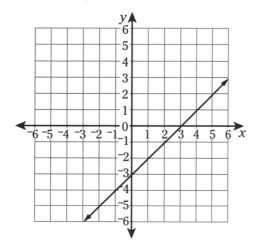

What are the slope and y-intercept of the graphed line?

A The slope is 1, and the y-intercept is 3.

B The slope is 1, and the y-intercept is -3.

C The slope is 3, and the y-intercept is 1.

D The slope is 3, and the y-intercept is -1.

2. A pole is placed against a house, 6 feet from the base of the wall. In this position, the pole has a slope of $\frac{5}{3}$. What height off the ground does the top of the pole rest against the house?

A 2.5 feet

B 5 feet

C 10 feet

D 30 feet

3. A snowstorm laid down more snow on top of an existing base. The equation below can be used to find the total inches of snow, s, on the ground after any number of hours, h, of the storm.

$$s = 0.75h + 4$$

What does the number 0.75 represent in the equation?

A the length of time in hours the snowstorm lasted

B the inches of snow that fell per hour during the storm

C the inches of snow on the ground after $\frac{3}{4}$ of an hour

D the inches of snow on the ground at the beginning of the storm

Read each problem. Circle the letter of the best answer.

4. The table below shows the rate charged to park in a parking garage.

Number of Hours	Cost to Park ($)
0.5	1.00
1.0	1.75
1.5	2.50
2.0	3.25

Melissa has parked her car in the garage for 2 hours already. How much more will it cost for her car to be parked for 1 additional hour?

A $0.75

B $1.00

C $1.50

D $1.75

5. What is the rate of change shown on the graph below?

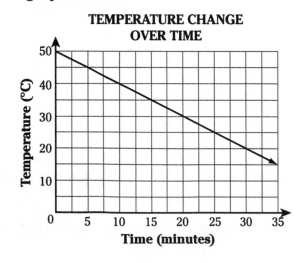

TEMPERATURE CHANGE OVER TIME

A −20°C per minute

B −10°C per minute

C −5°C per minute

D −1°C per minute

6. In which graph does the line have a slope of −2 and a y-intercept of 1?

A
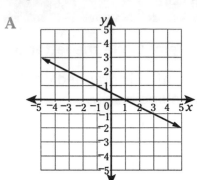

B
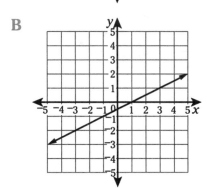

C
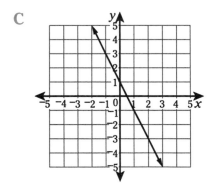

D
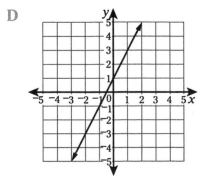

Read each problem. Circle the letter of the best answer.

7. A balloon is released into the air at a height of 25 meters, and rises at a rate of 1.4 meters per second. Which expression gives the number of seconds the balloon will take to reach a height of 80 meters?

   A 1.4(80) − 25

   B 1.4(80) + 25

   C 1.4(80 − 25)

   D 1.4(80 + 25)

8. Dimitri is buying a camera on an installment plan. He makes equal monthly payments. The equation below can be used to find the amount he owes after any number of months of payments.

   $$y = -25x + 400$$

   What does the number 400 represent in the equation?

   A the total cost of the camera

   B the amount Dimitri pays each month

   C the amount Dimitri put down as a deposit

   D the number of months Dimitri will make payments

9. Two trains are approaching Chicago. The graph shows how each train's distance to Chicago is changing over time.

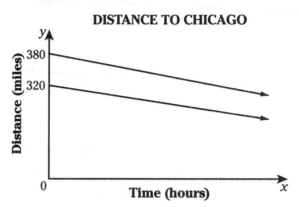

DISTANCE TO CHICAGO

The slope of the line describing train 1 has slope –60. The slope of the line describing train 2 has slope –50. Which statement best compares the two trains' expected arrival times in Chicago?

   A Train 1 will arrive 4 minutes before train 2.

   B Train 1 will arrive 6.7 minutes before train 2.

   C Train 2 will arrive 6 minutes before train 1.

   D Train 2 will arrive 3.3 minutes before train 1.

Writing Linear Equations

A1.2.2.1.3, A1.2.2.1.4

Forms of a Linear Equation

Linear equations can be represented in these ways:

- **Standard Form**

    $ax + by = c$, with constants a, b, and c, and a and b are not both zero

    Example: $4x - y = 3$ $a = 4, b = -1, c = 3$

- **Point-Slope Form**

    $(y - y_1) = m(x - x_1)$, with slope m and point (x_1, y_1)

    Example: $y - 5 = \frac{2}{3}(x + 9)$ $m = \frac{2}{3}$, point $(-9, 5)$

- **Slope-Intercept Form**

    $y = mx + b$, with slope m and y-intercept b

    Example: $y = -2x - 6$ $m = -2, b = -6$

For an equation written in standard form or point-slope form, the slope and y-intercept can be identified by rewriting the equation in slope-intercept form. For example, $6x + 3y = 4$ can be written in slope-intercept form by solving the equation for y.

$$3y = -6x + 4$$

$$y = -2x + \frac{4}{3}$$

The slope of this equation is -2 and the y-intercept is $\frac{4}{3}$.

Try this sample question.

S-1 What is the y-intercept in the equation $y - 3 = 4(x - 2)$?

A -8 B -5 C -3 D -2

This equation is written in point-slope form. Rewrite it in $y = mx + b$, or slope-intercept, form. Then look for the last value in the equation corresponding to b, the y-intercept.

$$y - 3 = 4(x - 2)$$
$$y - 3 = 4x - 8 \qquad \text{Distribute 4.}$$
$$y = 4x - 5 \qquad \text{Add 3 to both sides.}$$

The equation $y = 4x - 5$ is written in slope-intercept form. The last value in this equation is -5, so the y-intercept is -5. Choice B is correct.

Finding Intercepts from Equations

Recall that the *x*-intercept of a line is the point where the line touches the *x*-axis. The *y*-value at this point is 0. The point $(a, 0)$ describes the *x*-intercept. Similarly, the *y*-intercept of a line is the point where the line touches the *y*-axis. The *x*-value at this point is 0. The point $(0, b)$ describes the *y*-intercept.

To find the *x*-intercept of a line given its equation, substitute 0 for *y* and solve for *x*. To find the *y*-intercept of a line given its equation, substitute 0 for *x* and solve for *y*. For example, look at the equation $y = 2x + 8$.

x-intercept: let $y = 0$

$$0 = 2x + 8$$
$$-8 = 2x$$
$$-4 = x$$

x-intercept $= -4 = (-4, 0)$

y-intercept: let $x = 0$

$$y = 2(0) + 8$$
$$y = 8$$

y-intercept $= 8 = (0, 8)$

Try this sample question.

S-2 What is the *x*-intercept of the line having the equation below?

$$3x - 5y = -15$$

A $(-5, 0)$ B $(0, -3)$ C $(0, 3)$ D $(5, 0)$

The *x*-intercept occurs when $y = 0$. To find the *x*-intercept, substitute 0 for *y* and solve for *x*:

$$3x - 5y = -15$$
$$3x - 5(0) = -15 \qquad \text{Substitute } y = 0.$$
$$3x = -15 \qquad \text{Simplify.}$$
$$x = -5 \qquad \text{Divide both sides by 3.}$$

The *x*-intercept is the point $(-5, 0)$. Choice A is correct.

Finding the Equation of a Line from a Graph

If you are given the graph of a line, the equation of the line can be found using the slope-intercept formula.

- **Slope-Intercept Formula for a Line:** If a line has slope *m* and intersects the *y*-axis at $(0, b)$, then the equation of the line is $y = mx + b$.

For example, the line shown here intersects the *y*-axis at $(0, 3)$. Therefore, $b = 3$. You can use the points $(0, 3)$ and $(4, 1)$ to find the slope.

$$\frac{y_2 - y_1}{x_2 - x_1} = \frac{1 - 3}{4 - 0} = \frac{-2}{4} = -\frac{1}{2}$$

Therefore, the equation of the line in slope-intercept form is:

$$y = -\frac{1}{2}x + 3$$

An advantage of slope-intercept form is that the equation of the line is already solved for *y*.

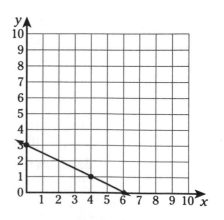

Try this sample question.

S-3 Which of these graphs represents the line $3x + 2y = -2$?

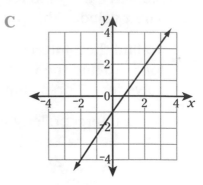

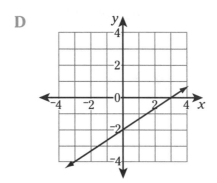

The equation $3x + 2y = -2$ is written in standard form. Rewrite the equation in slope-intercept form by solving for y:

$$2y = -3x - 2$$

$$y = -\frac{3}{2}x - 1$$

The slope, m, is $-\frac{3}{2}$ and the y-intercept, b, is -1. Only the graphs in choices A and C have a y-intercept of -1. The slope of the graph in choice C is $+\frac{3}{2}$, and the slope of the graph in choice A is $-\frac{3}{2}$. Choice A is correct.

Finding the Equation of a Line from Two Points

Given the coordinates of any two points, you can find the equation of that line using the point-slope formula.

- **Point-Slope Formula for a Line:** If a line goes through the point (x_1, y_1) and has slope m, then the equation of the line is $y - y_1 = m(x - x_1)$.

When using the point-slope formula, you will also need to use the formula for slope.

The slope formula is
$$m = \frac{y_2 - y_1}{x_2 - x_1}.$$

For example, here is how to find the equation for the line that goes through $(2, 3)$ and $(4, 7)$, as shown on the graph.

First use the slope formula to find the slope. You can let $(x_2, y_2) = (4, 7)$ and $(x_1, y_1) = (2, 3)$.

$$\frac{y_2 - y_1}{x_2 - x_1} = \frac{7 - 3}{4 - 2} = \frac{4}{2} = 2$$

Next use the point-slope formula with the known values of m, x_1, and y_1. The slope, m, is 2.

$$y - y_1 = m(x - x_1)$$
$$y - 3 = 2(x - 2)$$

Finally you can solve for y to rewrite this equation in the more common slope-intercept form.

$$y - 3 = 2(x - 2)$$
$$y - 3 = 2x - 4$$
$$y - 3 + 3 = 2x - 4 + 3$$
$$y = 2x - 1$$

Try this sample question.

S-4 Which equation represents the line that passes through the points $(2, -1)$ and $(3, 3)$?

A $y = 2x - 3$ C $y = 4x - 3$

B $y = 2x - 9$ D $y = 4x - 9$

First find the slope of the line:

$$m = \frac{y_2 - y_1}{x_2 - x_1} = \frac{3 - (-1)}{3 - 2} = 4$$

Next use the point-slope formula with slope 4 and known point $(3, 3)$. So $y - 3 = 4(x - 3)$. Rewrite the equation by solving for y:

$$y - 3 = 4x - 12$$
$$y = 4x - 9$$

Choice D is correct.

Finding the Equation of a Line from the Slope and a Point

The point-slope form of a line can also be used to find the equation of a line when the slope and only one point on the line are known. For example, suppose a line has a slope of 5 and contains the point $(-1, 4)$. Using the point-slope formula, the equation of the line would be:

$$y - y_1 = m(x - x_1)$$
$$y - 4 = 5(x + 1)$$
$$y - 4 = 5x + 5$$
$$y = 5x + 9$$

Try this sample question.

S-5 The temperature of a liquid cools 4°F every minute. After 5 minutes, the temperature of the liquid is 175°F. Which equation best models the temperature, y, of this liquid after x minutes?

A $y = -4x + 155$

B $y = -4x + 195$

C $y = -5x + 155$

D $y = -5x + 195$

Slope represents the rate of change. The slope of this line, then, is -4 since the temperature decreases (cools) 4 degrees each minute. A point on this line is $(5, 175)$. Use the point-slope formula with slope -4 and known point $(5, 175)$. So, $y - 175 = -4(x - 5)$.

Rewrite the equation in terms of y, that is, in slope-intercept form:

$y - 175 = -4x + 20$

$y = -4x + 195$

Choice B is correct.

Read each problem. Circle the letter of the best answer.

1. A graph of a linear equation is shown below.

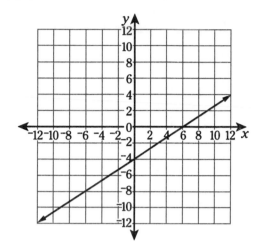

Which equation describes the graph?

A $y = \frac{3}{2}x + 4$

B $y = \frac{2}{3}x + 4$

C $y = \frac{3}{2}x - 4$

D $y = \frac{2}{3}x - 4$

2. Which statement is true of the equation below?

$$y - 6 = -3(x + 1)$$

A The slope is 3 and the y-intercept is 1.

B The slope is 3 and the y-intercept is -6.

C The slope is -3 and the y-intercept is 1.

D The slope is -3 and the y-intercept is 3.

3. The air pressure in a tire is 45 pounds per square inch (psi). Air is released at a constant rate until the tire is deflated. The graph below shows the air pressure (y) in the tire after x minutes.

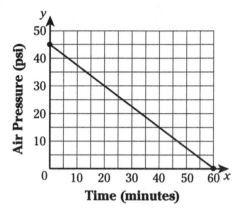

Which of these equations represents the relationship between time and the air pressure?

A $y = \frac{3}{4}x + 45$

B $y = \frac{3}{4}x - 45$

C $y = -\frac{3}{4}x + 45$

D $y = -\frac{3}{4}x - 45$

Read each problem. Circle the letter of the best answer.

4. Which graph shows the line $y + 2 = \frac{3}{2}x$?

   A

   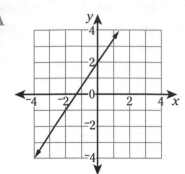

   B

   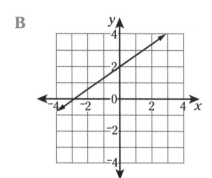

   C

   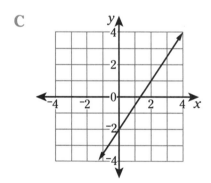

   D

   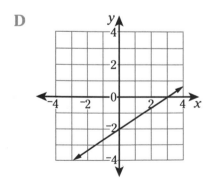

5. Which is an equation of the line that contains the points $(0, 3)$ and $(-2, 4)$?

   A $2x + y = 3$

   B $x + 2y = 6$

   C $2x + y = 0$

   D $x - 2y = 6$

6. A line contains the point $(-3, -1)$ and has a slope of $\frac{1}{3}$. Which equation represents this line?

   A $x + 3y = 0$

   B $x - 3y = 0$

   C $3x + y = 0$

   D $3x - y = 0$

7. A musician charges \$45 per hour to play at a party, plus a certain set-up fee. Her total charge for playing 3 hours is \$223. Which equation describes the relationship between x, the time in hours she plays, and y, the total charge in dollars?

   A $y + 3 = 45(x + 223)$

   B $y - 3 = 45(x - 223)$

   C $y + 223 = 45(x + 3)$

   D $y - 223 = 45(x - 3)$

Read each problem. Circle the letter of the best answer.

8. Which is an equation of the line that contains the points $(0, 2)$ and $(4, 0)$?

   A $x + 2y = 4$

   B $x - 2y = 4$

   C $2x + y = 4$

   D $2x - y = 4$

9. A company noticed a linear relationship between the price of a luggage set and the number of luggage sets sold. At $100, the company sold 1,000 sets. When the company raised the price to $120, they sold 800 sets. Which equation relates the price of the luggage sets to the total number of luggage sets sold?

   A $y - 100 = 10(x - 1{,}000)$

   B $y - 1{,}000 = 10(x - 100)$

   C $y - 100 = -10(x - 1{,}000)$

   D $y - 1{,}000 = -10(x - 100)$

10. Slices of cheese pizza cost $3 each, and slices of gourmet pizza cost $4 each. A soccer coach will spend a total of $48 on slices of pizza for his team. The equation below shows the relationship between x, the number of slices of cheese pizza, and y, the number of slices of gourmet pizza the coach will buy.

    $$3x + 4y = 48$$

    If the coach does not buy any slices of cheese pizza, how many slices of gourmet pizza can he buy?

    A 3

    B 4

    C 12

    D 16

Equations of Lines of Best Fit

A1.2.2.2.1

Identifying Lines of Best Fit

Linear equations are often used to model real-life relationships. However, real-life data does not always fall neatly along a well-defined line.

A **scatter plot** displays data corresponding to two variables at once. In the example below, each point represents the distance in miles a commuter lives from work and the time in minutes that person spends commuting. For example, the point at $(6, 16)$ represents a person who lives 6 miles from work and takes 16 minutes to commute there.

Although the data do not form a straight line, you can imagine a trend line sloping upward and to the right that comes fairly close to each data point. This is a **line of best fit.** A line of best fit goes through the points on a scatter plot. The distance between the line and all points above it is the same as the distance between the line and all points below it. The line does not have to pass through the actual points.

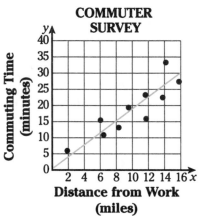

Try this sample question.

S-1   A set of data points is shown below.

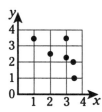

Which graph shows a line that best fits the data?

A 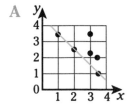   B 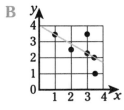   C 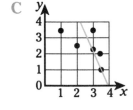   D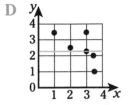

The line of best fit is the line closest to all data points. In choice A, some points are above the line but none are below it. In choice C, points above the line are much closer than points below it. In choice D, the line is not close to many points. Only choice B shows a line that is close to many points and equidistant from points above and below it. Choice B is correct.

Finding an Equation of a Line of Best Fit

A line sketched through the points of a scatter plot is a trend line, an approximate line of best fit. To find the **equation of the line of best fit,** you can enter points from the graph into a graphing calculator and output a regression line. Or, you can identify two points on the line and find the equation by hand.

Sometimes a line of best fit is known as a **regression line.**

In the example at right, the points $(1, 45)$ and $(4.5, 75)$ are on the trend line. To find the equation of the line of best fit, first determine the slope using the slope formula and the points:

$$m = \frac{y_2 - y_1}{x_2 - x_1} = \frac{75 - 45}{4.5 - 1} = \frac{30}{3.5} \approx 8.6$$

The slope of the equation of the line of best fit is 8.6.

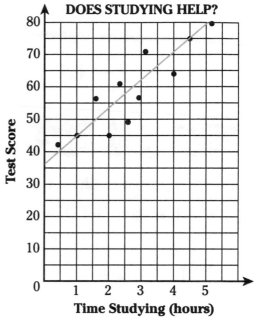

Now substitute the slope value and the value of the first point, $(1, 45)$, into slope-intercept form and solve to find b, the y-intercept value:

$$y = mx + b$$
$$45 = 8.6(1) + b$$
$$36.4 = b$$

Use the slope and y-intercept value to write the equation of the line of best fit: $y = 8.6x + 36.4$.

Try this sample question.

S-2 The scatter plot shows the relationship between the average temperature at a sports stadium and bottled water sales. Which of the following is the equation of the line of best fit?

A $\quad y = 0.11x - 1.15$

B $\quad y = 0.11x + 1.15$

C $\quad y = 9.17x - 9.98$

D $\quad y = 9.17x + 9.98$

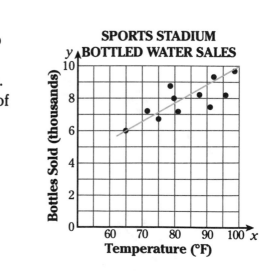

Select two points on the line: $(65, 6)$ and $(98, 9.6)$. Then calculate the slope:

$$m = \frac{9.6 - 6.0}{98 - 65} = \frac{3.6}{33} = 0.10909\ldots \approx 0.11$$

Use the slope and the value of a point to find the y-intercept:

$$6 = 0.11(65) + b$$
$$6 = 7.15 + b$$
$$-1.15 = b$$

So, the equation of the line of best fit in slope-intercept form is $y = 0.11x - 1.15$. Choice A is correct.

IT'S YOUR TURN

Read each problem. Circle the letter of the best answer.

1. Which scatter plot shows a line of best fit?

   A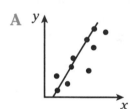

   B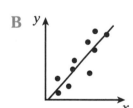

   C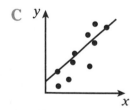

   D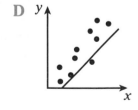

2. The scatter plot below shows the relationship between the heights of office buildings downtown and the number of floors in each office building.

   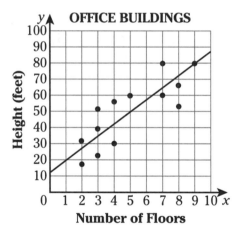

   Which equation best represents the line of best fit for this data?

   A $y = \frac{2}{15}x + 12.5$

   B $y = \frac{3}{4}x + 12.5$

   C $y = \frac{4}{3}x + 12.5$

   D $y = \frac{15}{2}x + 12.5$

Read each problem. Circle the letter of the best answer.

3. The scatter plot below shows how the number of baseball caps sold each day at a tourist shop is related to the cost per baseball cap.

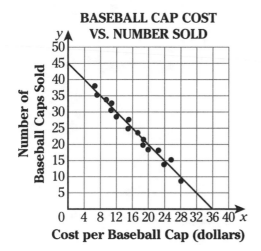

Which equation **best** describes the line of best fit?

A $y = -\frac{4}{5}x + 36$

B $y = -\frac{4}{5}x + 45$

C $y = -\frac{5}{4}x + 36$

D $y = -\frac{5}{4}x + 45$

4. The scatter plot below shows the relationship between the weight in tons of an SUV and the SUV's average fuel efficiency in miles per gallon.

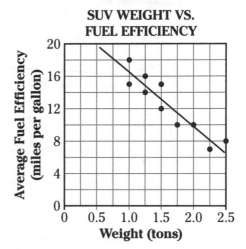

Which equation models the line of best fit?

A $y = 0.15x + 2.7$

B $y = -0.15x + 2.7$

C $y = 6.7x + 23$

D $y = -6.7x + 23$

Read the problem. Circle the letter of the best answer.

5. The scatter plot below shows how the school record in the girls' 100-meter run has changed over a period of 50 years.

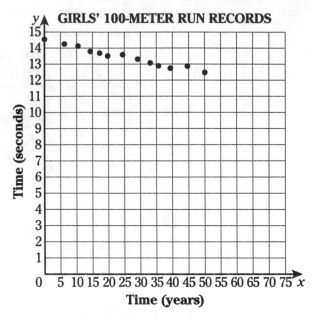

Lily drew the line of best fit on the scatter plot. Which equation **best** approximates the line of best fit?

A $y = -0.02x + 12.5$

B $y = -0.02x + 14.5$

C $y = -0.04x + 12.5$

D $y = -0.04x + 14.5$

Read the problem. Write your answer for each part.

1. There is a linear relationship between the number of people in a group and the cost to enter a museum. The museum charges $20 for two people and $28 for three people.

   A Write the equation in slope-intercept form that relates the number of people in a group to the cost of entering the museum. Show your work.

   Answer: _____

   B How much will it cost for a single individual to enter the museum?

   Answer: _____

   C How many people can enter the museum for $100?

   Answer: _____

Read the problem. Write your answer for each part.

2. The bottom of a ramp is placed 15 feet from the edge of a stage platform. The ramp is 3 feet off the ground when it is 10 feet from the edge of the stage.

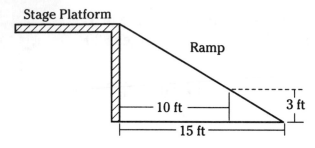

A What is the slope of the ramp? Show your work.

Answer: _____

B How many feet off the ground is the top of the ramp?

Answer: _____

C Write a linear equation in slope-intercept form that represents the height (*y*) of the ramp at any distance (*x*) from the stage.

Answer: _____

Read the problem. Write your answer for each part.

3. Ashley is the manager of a theater. She has $240 to spend on posters to advertise a new play. Ashley can spend exactly $240 to print 48 small posters. She can also spend exactly $240 to print 30 large posters.

   A Write an equation that can be used to find all combinations of small posters (x) and large posters (y) that will cost exactly $240.

   Answer: _____

   B Graph your equation from **part A** below.

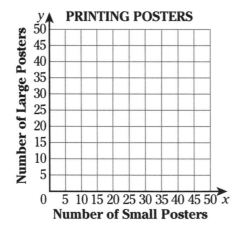

Unit 6 Coordinate Geometry

C What is the slope of the line you graphed in **part B?**

Answer: _____

D Explain what the slope from **part C** means in this situation.

Read the problem. Write your answer for each part.

4. The scatter plot below shows the age and length of 20 alligators.

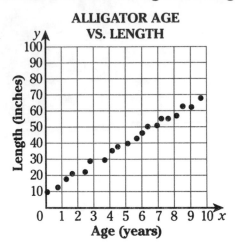

ALLIGATOR AGE VS. LENGTH

A Draw the line of best fit on the scatter plot above.

B Write an equation that describes the line of best fit.

Answer: _____

C Explain how you found your equation in **part B.**

D Explain the meaning of the slope of the line in this situation.

Read the problem. Write your answer for each part.

5. A kitchen sink is draining very slowly. The graph shows how the amount of water in the sink is changing over time.

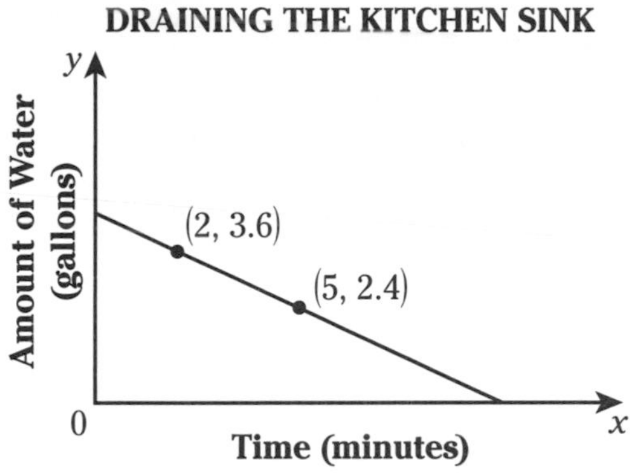

DRAINING THE KITCHEN SINK

A Find the slope of the line in the graph.

Answer: _____

B Write an equation of the line in point-slope form.

Answer: _____

C Find the *x*- and *y*-intercepts of the line.

Answer: _____ and _____

D Explain the meaning of the *x*- and *y*-intercepts in this situation.

Read the problem. Write your answer for each part.

6. Neil gets in an elevator at the 30th floor, and it begins to move downward at a speed of 8 feet per second. After 12 seconds, the elevator is 240 feet above the ground.

   A Let y = the height in feet of the elevator x seconds after Neil got in. Write an equation to show the relationship between x and y.

   Answer: _____

   B Explain how you found your equation in **part A.**

   C Use your equation to find the height of the elevator when Neil got in.

   Answer: _____

   D Use your equation to find how long it will take the elevator to reach ground level.

   Answer: _____

Module 2
Linear Functions and Data Organizations

Unit 7
Data Analysis

Central Tendency and Dispersion

A1.2.3.1.1, A1.2.3.2.2

When you read a magazine, watch sports, or surf the Internet, you will often encounter statements like "car sales this month are slower than expected" or "Rogers is the best player in the league right now." Statements like these present conclusions based on data. Frequently, these conclusions are derived from a **measure of central tendency,** that is, a number that marks a "middle" of the data.

Mean, Median, and Mode

The three most important measures of central tendency are mean, median, and mode.

- The **mean** is the sum of the data values divided by the number of values.

> The mean is also called the **average.**

- The **median** is the number in the middle of a set of data values.

- The **mode** is the value that occurs most often in a set of data values.

For example, assume that the girls' soccer team scored 0, 2, 6, 1, and 3 goals in its last five games. Then, the mean number of goals scored is $\frac{0 + 2 + 6 + 1 + 3}{5} = \frac{12}{5} = 2.4$. To find the median score, place the scores in order and locate the score in the middle: 0, 1, 2, 3, 6. The median score is 2. This set of data has no mode because every score occurs only once. If the team plays a sixth game and scores 1 goal, then the mode of the six games would be 1 because 1 would occur twice in the set of data.

Try this sample question.

S-1 The selling prices of 5 houses in one neighborhood were $114,000, $150,000, $223,000, $198,000, and $139,000. Which conclusion is true?

   A The mean price was about $15,000 higher than the median price.

   B The median price was about $15,000 higher than the mean price.

   C The mean and median prices were identical.

   D The mean price was double the median price.

Find the mean by adding the prices and dividing by 5: $114,000 + $150,000 + $223,000 + $198,000 + $139,000 = $824,000; $824,000 ÷ 5 = $164,800. The mean price is $164,800. Find the median by arranging the prices in order: $114,000, $139,000, $150,000, $198,000, $223,000. The median price is $150,000. Compare the mean and median: $164,800 is $14,800 more than $150,000. So choice A is correct.

Range

While mean, median, and mode are measures of central tendency, **range** is a measure of **dispersion,** or spread. When the range of a set of data is large, the data are very spread out. When the range is small, the data are very close together. To compute range, find the difference between the highest and lowest numbers in a data set.

Among the 30 people at a picnic, the youngest person is 3 years old, and the oldest person is 79 years old. Then the range of the ages is 79 − 3 = 76. At another picnic, the youngest person is 10 years old, and the range is 21. What can you say about the oldest person? That person must be 31 because 10 + 21 = 31.

> Arranging the numbers in order or making a tally chart can help you find the range.

Try this sample question.

S-2 A company asked 7 employees to turn in receipts for their travel expenses. The expenses were separated into transportation (plane travel, car rental, taxi) and lodging (hotel rooms, meals).

TRAVEL EXPENSES

Employee	Transportation	Lodging
Watkins	$460	$534
Sawamura	$912	$350
Jensen	$794	$483
Stolzfus	$329	$311
McManus	$409	$612
Escobar	$211	$543
Chang	$902	$433

A Which was more spread out, the transportation expenses or the lodging expenses? Justify your answer.

B The company is planning to send another employee on a business trip. About how much money, in all, should the company expect the employee to spend on the trip? Explain how you determined the answer.

For part A, the best way to measure spread is to calculate the range. The range of transportation costs is $912 − $211 = $701. The range of lodging costs is $612 − $311 = $301. Therefore, the transportation costs are more spread out.

For part B, one way to predict how much it will cost to send another employee on a business trip is to use medians. The median transportation cost in the table is $460. The median lodging cost in the table is $483. Combined, the total is $460 + $483 = $943. The company should expect to spend about $943 for the employee's business trip.

Quartiles and Interquartile Range

Quartiles and interquartile range are more difficult to work with and understand than mean, median, mode, and range, but they provide important ways of summarizing data. You should be sure that you are comfortable with mean, median, mode, and range before attempting to understand quartiles and interquartile range.

Because the median is the middle number in a set of data, you can think of the median as dividing the data into two halves, a lower half and an upper half. Frequently, people who use statistics decide that it is also valuable to divide data into fourths. When data are divided into fourths, the divisions between the groups of data are called **quartiles.**

- The **first quartile** is the median of the lower half of the data.
- The **second quartile** is the median of all of the data.
- The **third quartile** is the median of the upper half of the data.
- The **interquartile range** is the range between the third and first quartiles.

The following data set of seven numbers helps illustrate this.

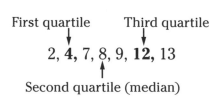

There are an odd number of values, so the median, or second quartile, is the number in the middle, 8. To divide the set into equal halves, discard the median. Now the lower and upper halves each have three values. The median of the lower half is 4; this is the first quartile of the set. The median of the upper half is 12; this is the third quartile. The interquartile range is 12 − 4 = 8.

Whenever the set or the upper and lower halves of a set contain an even number of values, you must calculate the median. In such cases, the calculated value may not actually be a number in the set. Look at this set of six values.

First quartile   Third quartile

3, **6**, 9, 10, **10**, 11

9.5

Second quartile

The second quartile, 9.5, is not actually a number in the set. It is the mean of the two middle numbers: $(9 + 10) \div 2 = 9.5$. Since it is not actually part of the set, it does not need to be discarded to find the medians of the lower and upper halves. There are already an equal number of values in the halves.

Sometimes all three quartiles need to be calculated.

The quartiles and interquartile range lead to various statements that can be made about data:

- Roughly one-fourth of data fall below the first quartile.

- Roughly one-fourth of data fall above the third quartile.

- Roughly one-half of data (the middle 50%) fall between the first and third quartiles.

- The interquartile range is a measure of how spread out the middle 50% of the data are.

Try this sample question.

S-3 A scientist recorded the temperature, in degrees Celsius, in 12 different parts of a rainforest. Her results are shown below.

11, 14, 12, 15, 8, 16, 21, 10, 11, 17, 13, 10

What is the interquartile range, in degrees Celsius, of the temperatures?

A 0.5   B 2.0   C 4.5   D 5.0

First arrange the temperatures in order from least to greatest.

8, 10, 10, 11, 11, 12, 13, 14, 15, 16, 17, 21

Since there are an even number of data points, the median is found by taking the mean of the middle two data points.

$$\frac{12 + 13}{2} = 12.5$$

The median of the data is 12.5.

To find the first quartile, take the median of the lower half of the data. The lower half of the data are the values below 12.5.

8, 10, 10, 11, 11, 12

$$\frac{10 + 11}{2} = 10.5$$

The median of these numbers, the first quartile, is 10.5.

To find the third quartile, take the median of the upper half of the data. The upper half of the data are all the values above 12.5.

13, 14, 15, 16, 17, 21

$$\frac{15 + 16}{2} = 15.5$$

The median of these numbers, the third quartile, is 15.5.

Finally, find the interquartile range by subtracting the first quartile from the third quartile.

15.5 − 10.5 = 5.0

The interquartile range is 5.0. Choice D is correct.

IT'S YOUR TURN

Read each problem. Circle the letter of the best answer.

1. A marine biologist weighed sea otters. The results are shown below.

SEA OTTER WEIGHTS

Sea Otter	Weight (pounds)
1	70.1
2	99.0
3	85.9
4	79.4
5	73.8
6	62.7

What is the median sea otter weight?

A 76.6 pounds

B 78.5 pounds

C 79.4 pounds

D 82.7 pounds

2. The scores Terrence got in the last ten video games he played are listed below.

400   900   −250   −150   500
650   1,200   −100   1,350   950

What is the range of these scores?

A 1,100

B 1,200

C 1,500

D 1,600

Read each problem. Circle the letter of the best answer.

3. The table below shows the area, in square miles, of 11 U.S. territories.

U.S. TERRITORIES

Territory	Area (sq mi)
Puerto Rico	3,515
Guam	212
U.S. Virgin Islands	136
American Samoa	77
Northern Mariana Islands	184
Midway Islands	2
Wake Island	3
Johnston Atoll	1
Baker, Howland, and Jarvis Islands	1
Kingman Reef	1
Navassa Island	2

What is the third quartile of the data shown?

A 136 square miles

B 145 square miles

C 184 square miles

D 212 square miles

4. Eight judges rated a movie on a scale of 1 to 10. Their ratings are given below.

6, 8, 9, 10, 6, 9, 9, 8

What was the mode of the ratings?

A 4

B 6

C 8

D 9

5. This bar graph shows how much Day's Market Stand earned in 2012.

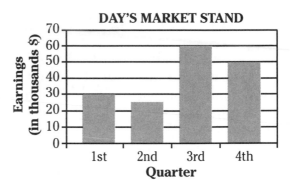

DAY'S MARKET STAND

What is the mean amount Day's Market Stand earned per quarter in 2012?

A $38,000

B $41,250

C $44,500

D $49,000

6. The prices of the five most popular big screen television sets at an electronics store are listed below.

$2,499 $1,359 $2,299
$2,999 $1,789

If the price of the next most popular television set is included with this data, the range in prices increases by $800. What could be the price of the next most popular television set?

A $2,159

B $2,199

C $3,799

D $3,859

Read each problem. Circle the letter of the best answer.

7. Javier's scores in 7 basketball games are shown below.

   18, 15, 20, 14, 12, 17, 18

   Javier has one more game, and he wants to average 17 points for all 8 games. How many points does he need to score in his last game?

   A 14

   B 17

   C 20

   D 22

8. The hourly pay rates of employees at a bookstore are listed below.

$7.15	$7.50	$7.50	$7.75
$7.90	$8.00	$8.00	$8.00
$8.25	$8.60	$8.80	$9.00
$9.00	$10.20	$11.00	$11.15
$11.75	$16.00	$16.75	$19.25

   Which statement is **best** supported by this data?

   A One-fourth of the employees have an hourly pay rate less than $7.95.

   B Half of the employees have an hourly pay rate between $8.00 and $9.60.

   C One-fourth of the employees have an hourly pay rate greater than $11.15.

   D Half of the employees have an hourly pay rate between $8.85 and $19.25.

9. The median age of cars on a used car lot is 4 years. The interquartile range of the cars' ages is 7 years. Which statement is most likely to be true?

   A About 25% of the cars will be less than 4 years old.

   B About 25% of the cars will be more than 4 years old.

   C About 50% of the cars will be between 4 and 7 years old.

   D About 75% of the cars will be less than 8 years old.

10. Omer counted the number of characters in 60 text messages and recorded the data. He found that the lower quartile of the data was 31, the median was 55, and the upper quartile was 96. Which is the best estimate of the number of text messages that had between 31 and 55 characters?

    A 15

    B 24

    C 30

    D 45

Predictions from Data

A1.2.3.2.1

Predictions Based on Trends

Data samples and trends found from data are often used to predict outcomes of larger populations or of future events. For example, this graph shows the amount of sales a company earned each year they were in business. This data can be used to predict the amount of sales they might expect to earn one year, two years, or five years into the future. From the trend in this data, a reasonable prediction might be that this company can expect to earn about $1,000,000 in sales by year 7.

Try this sample question.

S-1 The library formed a youth book club and an adult book club 5 years ago. The number of members in each book club is shown in the bar graph below.

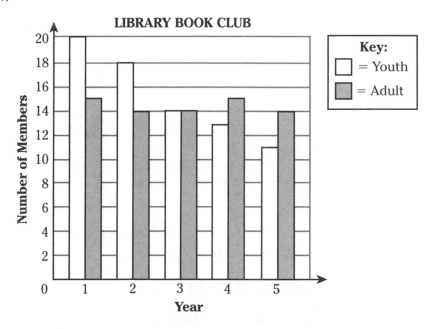

Assuming the trend in number of members in each book club continues, about how many total members would be expected in both book clubs by year 6?

A 8   B 14   C 22   D 28

From this data, the number of members in the youth book club tends to decrease by about 2 people each year. The number of members in the adult book club tends to remain the same from year to year. In year 5, there were about 11 members in the youth club. So, in year 6, about 11 − 2, or 9 members would be expected. The number of members in the adult club is about 14 each year. So, in year 6, the total number of expected members in both clubs is about 9 + 14 = 23. Of the choices, 22 is the closest. Choice C is correct.

Predictions Based on Probability

Predictions can be made on populations of data by finding probabilities of events occurring in samples. For example, the circle graph at right shows the responses of 50 people to a survey question.

RESPONSES TO SURVEY

The numbers tell you how many people chose *yes, no,* or *undecided.* There are 50 total responses and 15 out of 50, or 0.3, are *undecided.* This is the relative frequency. Therefore, if the survey is conducted with 600 people, you can predict that the number of people who are undecided would be 0.3 × 600 = 180 people.

Try this sample question.

S-2 The line plot below shows the ages of a sample of people at a movie theater.

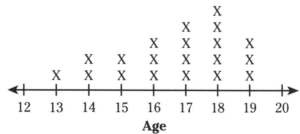

If there are 280 people in the theater, which prediction about the audience would you expect to be true?

A 50% will be younger than 16.

B 50% will be older than 18.

C About 70 people will be from 13 to 16 years old.

D About 210 people will be from 16 to 19 years old.

The line plot shows 20 data values and 15 of 20, or 75%, are stacked above the ages 16, 17, 18, and 19. If the audience consists of 280 people, then 75% of it could be expected to be from 16 to 19 years old: 0.75 × 280 = 210 people. Choice D is correct.

180

Read each problem. Circle the letter of the best answer.

1. The bar graph below shows the numbers of different kinds of animals adopted from a shelter one week.

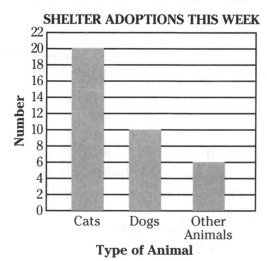

If 50 animals are adopted next week, which is the **best** estimate of the number of dogs that will be adopted?

A 10

B 14

C 20

D 28

2. The circle graph below shows the number of students at each grade level in one high school marching band.

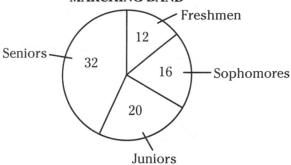

Hoshi is in the marching band. What is the likelihood that she is a senior?

A 32%

B 40%

C 52%

D 68%

Read each problem. Circle the letter of the best answer.

3. The line graph below shows how Gustav's hourly rate of pay changed during the past eight years.

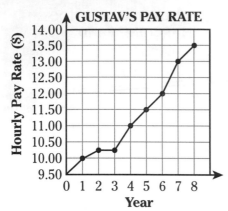

If Gustav stays in this job 10 years, what can he expect his hourly rate to be?

A $13.50

B $14.00

C $14.50

D $15.00

4. The line plot shows the heights of 20 randomly selected students at a high school.

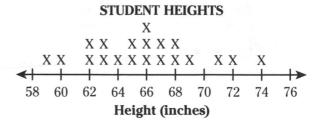

There are a total of 1,200 students at the high school. Which statement is the most reasonable conclusion from the data?

A Approximately 300 students at the school are 63 inches tall.

B Approximately 600 students at the school are 66 inches tall.

C Approximately 300 students at the school are more than 66 inches tall.

D Approximately 900 students at the school are more than 63 inches tall.

Read each problem. Circle the letter of the best answer.

5. Five students volunteer for a service project. The bar graph below shows the hours each student put in during the first month.

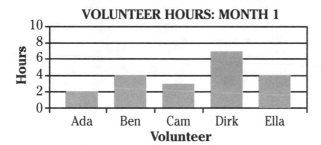

VOLUNTEER HOURS: MONTH 1

The project will continue for a total of 5 months. If the data in the graph is representative, how many more hours will Dirk have volunteered during the project than Ada?

A 10

B 15

C 25

D 35

6. The line graph shows the revenue from sales tax and income tax in one state over time.

Which is the **best** estimate of the expected difference between revenue from sales tax and income tax in 2020?

A $90 million

B $200 million

C $300 million

D $400 million

Read each problem. Circle the letter of the best answer.

7. Lisa asked 50 students in her school how many hours a week they work at an after-school job. The results of her survey are summarized in the circle graph below.

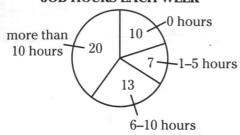

JOB HOURS EACH WEEK

There are 840 total students in Lisa's school. Based on the results of her survey, about how many total students in her school would be expected to work more than 10 hours a week?

A 168

B 200

C 336

D 400

8. Marcus asked 100 students to select the electronic device they valued the most. He graphed the results below.

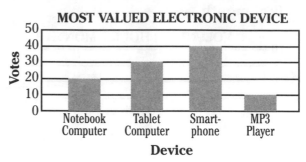

Marcus will ask another 50 students to select their most valued electronic device. Based on the information from the bar graph, how many more students of the next 50 will select the tablet computer rather than the notebook computer?

A 5

B 15

C 30

D 45

Representations of Data

A1.2.3.2.2

In an earlier lesson, you learned how to find the range, quartiles, and interquartile range of data. These measures are frequently used in certain data displays.

Box-and-Whisker Plots

One type of data display that uses quartiles is the **box-and-whisker plot.** Quartiles are used to create box-and-whisker plots as follows:

- The minimum value is the left-most whisker.
- The first quartile is the left edge of the box.
- The median (or second quartile) is the middle line in the box.
- The third quartile is the right edge of the box.
- The maximum value is the right-most whisker.

For example, the box-and-whisker plot below represents data with a median of 70 and an interquartile range of $85 - 50 = 35$.

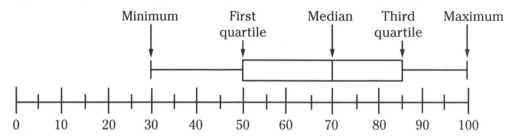

Try these sample questions.

S-1   The box-and-whisker plot below shows the number of touchdowns scored each year by a football player.

TOUCHDOWNS

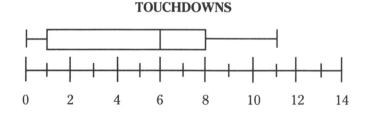

What was his median number of touchdowns?

A   1   B   6   C   8   D   11

In a box-and-whisker plot, the median is represented by the middle line in the box. This line matches up with 6 on the scale. The median number of touchdowns was 6. Choice B is correct.

Unit 7 Data Analysis

S-2 The box-and-whisker plot below shows the interest rates charged by credit card companies.

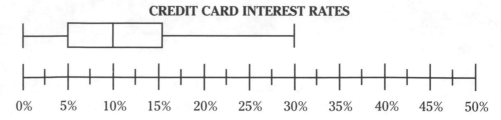

CREDIT CARD INTEREST RATES

0% 5% 10% 15% 20% 25% 30% 35% 40% 45% 50%

A Estimate the median interest rate charged by credit card companies. Explain how you found your answer.

B A credit card company that charges 6% interest claims that their rates are lower than 75% of all other credit card companies. Is this claim correct? Use mathematics to justify your answer.

For part A, locate the median. The median is the middle bar on the box-and-whisker plot. This appears to be at 10%. This means that half the interest rates are above 10%, and half the interest rates are below 10%.

For part B, notice that the company's claim that their rates are lower than 75%, or three-fourths, of all other credit card companies is equivalent to saying their rate falls below (or at) the first quartile of the data. You can see from the box-and-whisker plot that the first quartile of the data is at 5%. Since 6% is greater than 5%, the company's claim is incorrect.

Stem-and-Leaf Plots

Another way data can be organized is in a **stem-and-leaf plot.** To make a stem-and-leaf plot, the left digit or digits of all data values are lined up in the "stem" of the plot. The right digit of each individual data value is placed in the corresponding "leaf" of the stem.

For example, the ages of cast members in a play are 19, 35, 16, 24, 22, 37, 60, 34, 57, and 19. The stem-and-leaf plot shown here organizes these data values. Notice that the tens digits are the stem in this plot, and the individual ones digits are the leaves.

AGES OF CAST MEMBERS

1	6 9 9
2	2 4
3	4 5 7
4	
5	7
6	0

Key: 1 | 6 = 16

Measures of central tendency (mean, median, and mode) and measures of dispersion or spread (range and quartiles) can be determined based on the data in a stem-and-leaf plot. In the stem-and-leaf plot in the example, the first and last data values can be used to find the range: $60 - 16 = 44$. Also, the mode can be found by locating digits that repeat most often for a particular stem. The mode in this stem-and-leaf plot is 19 since there are two leaf 9's corresponding to the stem 1.

Try this sample question.

S-3 The stem-and-leaf plot below shows the number of copies made on the two copiers in the school library during a two-week period.

COPIES MADE EACH DAY

Copier 1		Copier 2
	2	
8 3	3	
9	4	8 9
2	5	1 6 6
1	6	
8 8 6 5	7	
2	8	0 4 8
	9	3
	10	7

Key: $52 = 2 \mid 5 \mid 1 = 51$

Which statement can be concluded from this data?

A The range for copier 1 is greater than the range for copier 2.

B The range for copier 2 is greater than the range for copier 1.

C The median for copier 1 is greater than the median for copier 2.

D The median for copier 2 is greater than the median for copier 1.

To find the range for each copier, first identify the smallest and largest data values. Remember that on a double stem-and-leaf plot, the left-hand values are read from *right to left*. The smallest value for copier 1 is 33 and the largest is 82. For copier 1, the range is $82 - 33 = 49$. For copier 2, the range is $107 - 48 = 59$. The range for copier 2 is greater than the range for copier 1. So choice B is correct.

Note that the median for each data set can be found by calculating the mean of the two middle values. The medians for the data sets are both 68, so the medians are equal.

Read each problem. Circle the letter of the best answer.

1. The algebra test scores from Ms. Grange's class are shown in the box-and-whisker plot below.

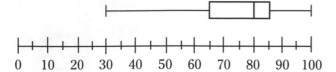

    What is the interquartile range of the algebra test scores?

    A 5

    B 15

    C 20

    D 25

2. Luke has 40 folders of digital pictures on his computer. The number of digital pictures in each folder is shown in the stem-and-leaf plot below.

    DIGITAL PICTURES PER FOLDER

    ```
    0 |
    1 | 3 5 6 6 8
    2 | 5 5 7
    3 | 0 2 4 4 4 8 8
    4 | 4 6 7 8 8
    5 | 0 0 2 2 2 2 5 7 9 9
    6 | 1 3 4 4 5 5
    7 | 0 2 4
    8 | 5
    ```

    Key: 1 | 3 = 13 pictures

    What is the median number of digital pictures Luke has stored per folder?

    A 34

    B 49

    C 52

    D 72

3. The stem-and-leaf plot below shows the length, in minutes, of each movie playing at the local theater complex this week.

    MOVIE LENGTHS

    ```
     8 | 8
     9 | 3 4 7 9
    10 | 0 8
    11 | 2 5 6 8 8
    12 | 0 4 5
    13 | 3
    ```

    Key: 8 | 8 = 88 minutes

    Which statement about the data is true?

    A The first quartile is 97.

    B The second quartile is 113.

    C The third quartile is 119.

    D The interquartile range is 22.

4. Zoe gathered information on annual car insurance rates in her area. These data are shown in the box-and-whisker plot below.

    ANNUAL CAR INSURANCE RATES ($)

    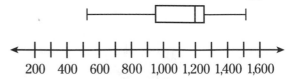

    Which amount is closest to the interquartile range of these rates?

    A $300

    B $525

    C $675

    D $950

Read each problem. Circle the letter of the best answer.

5. The box-and-whisker plot below shows the typing speed, in words per minute, of the students in Mr. Panko's typing class at the beginning of the year.

TYPING SPEED

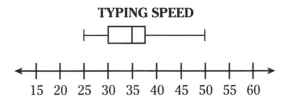

Based on this plot, which of the following statements must be true?

A   Exactly one student types 35 words per minute.

B   Exactly one student types 37 words per minute.

C   Half of the students type 35 words per minute or less.

D   Half of the students type 37 words per minute or less.

6. The box-and-whisker plot shows the distribution of prices for 25 digital cameras for sale at an electronics store.

CAMERA PRICES (dollars)

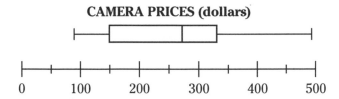

Which is the **best** estimate for the median of the data?

A $200

B $225

C $275

D $300

7. Jason and Stephen went fishing. The stem-and-leaf plot shows the lengths of the fish each boy caught.

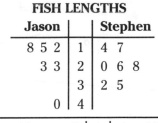

FISH LENGTHS

Jason		Stephen
8 5 2	1	4 7
3 3	2	0 6 8
	3	2 5
0	4	

Key: 12 cm = 2 | 1 | 4 = 14 cm

According to the data, if one more fish is caught, what is the probability it will be more than 30 centimeters long?

A $\frac{2}{7}$ C $\frac{2}{13}$

B $\frac{3}{10}$ D $\frac{3}{13}$

8. The box-and-whisker plot below shows the weight, in pounds, of each package a shipping company delivered one day.

PACKAGE WEIGHTS IN POUNDS

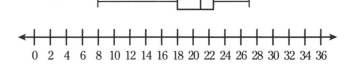

Which statement is **best** supported by the data in the box-and-whisker plot?

A   The median package weight was about 21 pounds.

B   The range in package weights was about 27 pounds.

C   More than half the packages weighed less than 18 pounds.

D   About one-fourth of the packages weighed between 21 and 27 pounds.

Read each problem. Circle the letter of the best answer.

9. The stem-and-leaf plot below shows the finish times, in seconds, of the top ten runners in a race.

RACE FINISH TIMES

30	2 8 8
31	4 6
32	0 5 5 6
33	
34	
35	
36	7

Key: 31 | 4 = 31.4 seconds

Which statement about the race times on the plot is true?

A The range of times is less than 6 seconds.

B The median time is exactly 1 second greater than the first quartile time.

C The third quartile time is more than 1 second greater than the median.

D The interquartile range of the times is more than 2 seconds.

10. A geologist recorded the masses of some rock samples in the stem-and-leaf plot below.

ROCK SAMPLE MASSES

1	5
2	2 6 7
3	
4	0 3 9
5	7
6	1 1 4

Key: 1 | 5 = 1.5 kilograms

Based on the data, which statement is most accurate?

A About 25% of the masses are less than 3 kilograms.

B About 50% of the masses are less than 4 kilograms.

C About 50% of the masses are between 2 and 6 kilograms.

D About 75% of the masses are less than 6 kilograms.

Predictions from Scatter Plots

A1.2.3.2.3

A scatter plot shows the relationship between two sets of data, which are written as ordered pairs and then graphed as points on a coordinate plane. A scatter plot can be used to identify trends, or correlations, in data. A line of best fit drawn through the points and its equation can model that relationship.

Predictions Based on Lines of Best Fit

In unit 6, lesson 3, you learned to draw a line of best fit on a scatter plot and write an equation for it, using two points on the line. Once a line of best fit is drawn, or its equation determined, you can make predictions.

Suppose that a researcher is studying the relationship between the number of telephones a family owns and the number of cars a family owns. His data are shown in the scatter plot at the right.

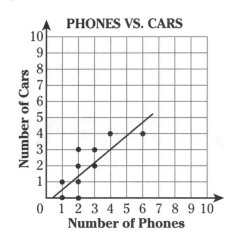

A line of best fit is given by the equation $y = 0.78x - 0.04$. The equation can be used to predict the number of cars owned by a family with 5 phones by substituting 5 for x and evaluating.

$$y = 0.78(5) - 0.04 = 3.86$$

Based on the line of best fit, a family with 5 phones should be expected to own 3.86 cars. Given the context of the problem, it probably makes sense to round this number up to 4.

Try this sample question.

S-1 The results of a survey of 8 engineers are given in the graph at the right.

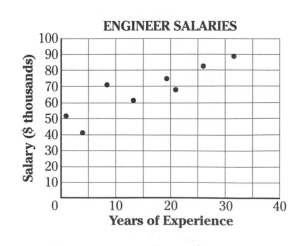

A Draw a line of best fit through the data.

B According to your line of best fit, what is the salary of an engineer with 15 years of experience? Explain how you found the answer.

For part A, you can calculate a line of best fit or you can simply "eyeball" a line of best fit. The important thing is that your line goes through the data reasonably well.

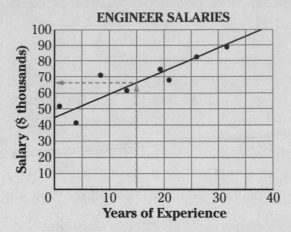

ENGINEER SALARIES

For part B, use the line of best fit to estimate the salary. The salary of an engineer with 15 years of experience is about $66,000.

IT'S YOUR TURN

Read each problem. Circle the letter of the best answer.

1. A scatter plot shows the relationship between the number of floors in office buildings downtown and the height of the buildings. The following equation models the line of best fit for the data.

$$y = \frac{15}{2}x + 10$$

What would be the expected height of a building with 20 floors?

A 155 feet

B 160 feet

C 225 feet

D 310 feet

2. This scatter plot relates the circumference and height of 10 trees.

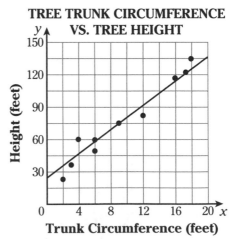

TREE TRUNK CIRCUMFERENCE VS. TREE HEIGHT

How tall would you expect a tree with a circumference of 8 feet to be?

A 65 feet

B 70 feet

C 75 feet

D 80 feet

Read each problem. Circle the letter of the best answer.

3. A certain model of car cost $20,000 when new. The scatter plot below shows the time since purchase and the value of 20 of these cars.

What will be the approximate value of one of these cars 6 years after purchase?

A $7,000

B $8,000

C $9,000

D $10,000

4. A scatterplot relates the weight, in pounds, of an order, to the charge, in dollars, to ship the order. The equation $y = 0.25x + 6$ describes the line of best fit. What would be the expected cost to ship a 50-pound order?

A $12.50

B $14.00

C $17.60

D $18.50

5. A scientist related the age and length of 20 baby sharks on this scatter plot.

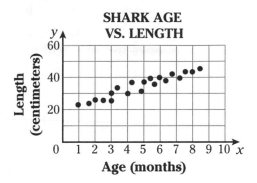

Based on the data, what would be the expected length of a 12-month old shark?

A 48 centimeters   C 53 centimeters

B 50 centimeters   D 56 centimeters

6. The scatter plot shows how a restaurant's monthly revenue is related to its monthly advertising expenditure.

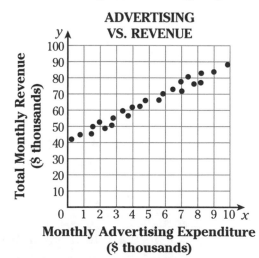

According to the equation of the line of best fit, what is the **best** prediction for revenue if the advertising expenditure is $18,000?

A $110,000   C $150,000

B $130,000   D $170,000

Probability of Compound Events

A1.2.3.3.1

A **compound event** involves two or more simple events occuring together. Examples of compound events include rolling two number cubes, flipping four coins, or scoring three baskets in a row. All of these probabilities involve more than one event.

> Probability of a simple event =
> $$\frac{\text{favorable outcomes}}{\text{total possible outcomes}}$$

Independent Events

When the probabilities of compound events do *not* influence each other, they are known as **independent events.**

- Probability of independent events A and B occurring:
  $P(A \text{ and } B) = P(A) \cdot P(B)$

The probability of event A occurring has no effect on the probability of event B occurring. For example, if two coins are flipped, the side the first coin lands on has no effect on the side that the second coin lands on. The probability that one coin lands on heads is $\frac{1}{2}$. The probability that both coins land on heads, then, is $\frac{1}{2} \cdot \frac{1}{2} = \frac{1}{4}$.

Try this sample question.

S-1 The spinner shown below is divided into 8 equal sections.

Constance spins the arrow on this spinner four times. What is the probability that the arrow lands on an even number all four times?

   A 0.0625   B 0.125   C 0.25   D 0.5

There are four even numbers on this spinner. If the arrow is spun once, the probability it lands on an even number is $\frac{4}{8}$ or $\frac{1}{2}$. If the arrow is spun four times, the probability it lands on an even number becomes $\frac{1}{2} \cdot \frac{1}{2} \cdot \frac{1}{2} \cdot \frac{1}{2} = \frac{1}{16}$. As a decimal, $\frac{1}{16} = 0.0625$. Choice A is correct.

Dependent Events

Sometimes the probabilities of compound events will influence each other. These events are known as **dependent events.** That is because the outcome of one event depends on the outcome of another event.

- Probability of dependent events A and B occurring:
  $P(A \text{ then } B) = P(A) \cdot P(B \text{ after } A \text{ occurs})$

The probability of event A occurring has an effect on the probability of event B occurring.

For example, suppose you have 5 quarters and 5 pennies in your wallet. You select two coins from the wallet without looking. If the first coin is not replaced, then the total number of coins in your wallet decreases from 10 to 9 after the first coin is selected. This has an effect on the probability of choosing the second coin.

Try these sample questions.

S-2 A bag contains the following letter tiles: 6 vowels and 10 consonants. Amanda selects three letter tiles from the bag without looking. She does not replace the letter tiles back in the bag. What is the probability that she selects all consonants?

    A $\dfrac{1}{2}$ **B** $\dfrac{5}{8}$ **C** $\dfrac{3}{14}$ **D** $\dfrac{125}{512}$

There are 16 total tiles before Amanda selects the first one: P(first tile a consonant) $= \dfrac{10}{16}$. Since the tile is not replaced, there are 15 total tiles left. Assuming the first tile selected was a consonant, then only 9 consonants are left. So, P(second tile a consonant) is $\dfrac{9}{15}$. Similarly, P(third tile a consonant) is $\dfrac{8}{14}$. The probability all three tiles selected are consonants is $\dfrac{10}{16} \cdot \dfrac{9}{15} \cdot \dfrac{8}{14} = \dfrac{3}{14}$. Choice C is correct.

S-3 From a group of 3 girls and 6 boys, two will be chosen to attend a conference. What percent chance is there that the first person chosen is a boy and the second person chosen is a girl?

    A 22%   **B** 25%   **C** 33%   **D** 50%

There are 9 total people. The probability that a boy is chosen first is P(boy) $= \dfrac{6}{9}$. Now there are 8 people remaining. The probability that a girl is chosen from the 8 remaining people is P(girl) $= \dfrac{3}{8}$. So, the probability of a boy being chosen first and then a girl being chosen second is P(boy then girl) $= \dfrac{6}{9} \cdot \dfrac{3}{8} = \dfrac{18}{72} = \dfrac{1}{4} = 0.25 = 25\%$. Choice B is correct.

Read each problem. Circle the letter of the best answer.

1. There is a 10% chance it will rain on Saturday and a 30% chance it will rain on Sunday. What percent chance is there that it will rain on both Saturday and Sunday?

   A 3%

   B 15%

   C 20%

   D 40%

2. In a shipment of alarm clocks, the probability that one alarm clock is defective is 0.04. Charlie selects three alarm clocks at random. If he puts each clock back with the rest of the shipment before selecting the next one, what is the probability that all three alarm clocks would be defective?

   A 0.000064

   B 0.00012

   C 0.064

   D 0.12

3. Stefan rolls a 1–6 number cube and flips a coin. What is the probability he rolls a number less than 5 and the coin lands on tails?

   A $8\frac{1}{3}\%$

   B $33\frac{1}{3}\%$

   C $41\frac{2}{3}\%$

   D $66\frac{2}{3}\%$

4. A cafeteria has 5 turkey sandwiches, 6 cheese sandwiches, and 4 tuna sandwiches. There are two students in line and each will take a sandwich. What is the probability that the first student takes a cheese sandwich and the next student takes a turkey sandwich?

   A $\frac{1}{7}$

   B $\frac{1}{14}$

   C $\frac{2}{15}$

   D $\frac{2}{21}$

Read each problem. Circle the letter of the best answer.

5. Natasha has a bag of gift bows. The table below shows the colors of bows in the bag.

BAG OF GIFT BOWS

Color	Number
White	6
Gold	5
Red	4
Blue	7
Green	2
Pink	1

If Natasha picks bows at random, what percent chance is there that the first two gifts she wraps will have a white bow?

A 0.8%

B 5%

C 5.76%

D 24%

6. A builder has 8 lots available for sale.

   • 6 lots are greater than one acre.

   • 2 lots are less than one acre.

What is the probability that the next three lots sold will be greater than one acre?

A $\frac{3}{4}$

B $\frac{15}{28}$

C $\frac{27}{64}$

D $\frac{5}{14}$

7. Wade is playing darts. Each dart throw scores a certain number of points, depending on where on the dartboard it lands, as shown below. A throw that misses the dartboard completely is worth 0 points.

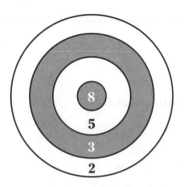

The table shows the probability of scoring 8, 5, 3, 2, or 0 points on any given throw.

DART SCORE PROBABILITIES

Score	Probability
8	0.1
5	0.2
3	0.3
2	0.3
0	0.1

If Wade throws two darts, what is the probability his total score will be exactly 10 points?

A 0.3

B 0.1

C 0.03

D 0.07

Read the problem. Write your answer for each part.

1. The box-and-whisker plot below shows students' scores on a practice driving test.

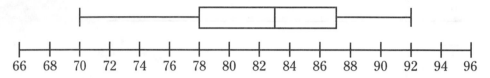

66 68 70 72 74 76 78 80 82 84 86 88 90 92 94 96

A What is the range of the scores?

Answer: _____

B What is the interquartile range?

Answer: _____

C If the plot represents 64 students, about how many scored
   above the third quartile?

   Answer: _____

D A passing score is 80. Explain how you know whether or not
   50% of the students passed the test.

Read the problem. Write your answer for each part.

2. Isaac's bowling scores for April are shown below. His mean score after all five games was 221.

ISAAC'S BOWLING SCORES

Game	1	2	3	4	5
Score	225	245	222	230	?

A What was Isaac's score in game 5?

Answer: _____

B What was Isaac's median score for the five games?

Answer: _____

C Isaac bowls a sixth game and his median score changes to 227.
What is Isaac's score on the sixth game?

Answer: _____

D Explain how you know your answer to **part C** is correct.

Read the problem. Write your answer for each part.

3. Brittney randomly selected 30 cars in a parking lot and determined each car's year of manufacture. She made this stem-and-leaf plot to show the results.

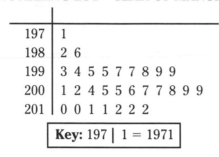

CARS IN PARKING LOT—YEAR OF MANUFACTURE

```
197 | 1
198 | 2 6
199 | 3 4 5 5 7 7 8 9 9
200 | 1 2 4 5 5 6 7 7 8 9 9
201 | 0 0 1 1 2 2 2
```

Key: 197 | 1 = 1971

A There are about 70,000 cars in the city where Brittney lives. According to Brittney's data, about how many of the cars in her city were manufactured before the year 2000?

Answer: _____

B Find the lower quartile and upper quartile of the data.

Answer: _____

C About how many of the cars in Brittney's city were manufactured between the years you found in **part B?**

Answer: _____

D Explain how you found your answer to **part C.**

Read the problem. Write your answer for each part.

4. The scatter plot shows the results of a study on the effects of exercise on resting heart rate.

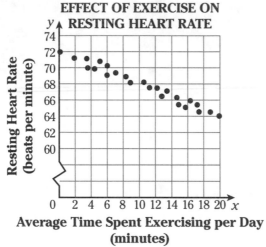

EFFECT OF EXERCISE ON RESTING HEART RATE

Resting Heart Rate (beats per minute)

Average Time Spent Exercising per Day (minutes)

A Draw the line of best fit on the scatter plot.

B Write the approximate equation of the line of best fit.

Answer: _____

C Use your equation to predict the resting heart rate of a person
who exercises 30 minutes per day.

Answer: _____

D Explain how you found your answer to **part C.**

Read the problem. Write your answer for each part.

5. There are 3 black marbles and 4 red marbles in a bag. Trevor will take out 2 marbles without looking.

   A What is the probability that both marbles will be black? Show your work.

   Answer: _____

   B Explain how you found your answer to **part A.**

   C Suppose that Trevor takes out 1 marble, replaces it in the bag, then takes out another marble. What is the probability that both marbles will be black in this situation? Show your work.

   Answer: _____

   D Explain how you found your answer to **part C.**

A

absolute value   the distance of a number from 0 on a number line

arithmetic pattern   a sequence of numbers that increases or decreases at a constant rate

B

binomial   a poly

box-and-whisker plot   a ....mmary and dispersion of a ....nd extremes

C

........ata by defining the typical

.... divided mentally, used to estimate

comp.....   .... of two or more simple events

compoun..... inequality   .... inequalities joined by the words *and* or *or*

cube root   .... of three equal factors (roots) of a number or expression; the .....nverse of cubing a number

D

dependent events   two or more events in which the outcome of one event influences the outcome of the other event(s)

difference of two squares   the product of the sum and difference of the same two terms; $(x + y)(x - y) = x^2 - y^2$

dispersion, measure of	a number that describes the spread of a set of data
domain	the set of all input, or x-, values of the independent variable in a relation

E

elimination	a method for solving a system of linear equations by adding or subtracting the equations to eliminate one variable, making it possible to solve for the other
equation of a line of best fit	a linear equation that models a line of best fit on a scatter plot, derived from two points on the line
estimate	an approximation based on a judgment
exponent	the power to which a number or expression is raised, that is, the number of times it is multiplied by itself

F

function	a relation in which each x-value is assigned to a unique y-value

G

graphing	a method for solving systems of equations by plotting the equations on a coordinate plane to find the point of intersection
greatest common factor (GCF)	the largest factor that two or more numbers or algebraic terms have in common
grouping, factoring by	to factor expressions with four or more terms to find binomial factors

I

independent events
two or more events in which the outcome of one event does not influence the outcome of the other event(s)

interquartile range
the difference between the first quartile and third quartile values in a set of data, representing the spread of 50% of the data

irrational number
a real number that cannot be expressed as the ratio of two integers; a non-terminating and non-repeating decimal

L

least common multiple (LCM)
the smallest number or expression that is a common multiple of two or more numbers or algebraic terms

line of best fit
a line drawn on a scatter plot to best estimate the relationship between two sets of data, showing the trend of the data

linear equation
an equation for which the graph is a straight line; an equation in which the variables are not multiplied by one another or raised to any power other than 1

linear function
a function whose graph is a straight line

linear inequality
a relation of two expressions using $>$, $<$, $\geq$, or $\leq$, whose boundary is a straight line and which has a range of solutions called a solution set

M

mapping
a method for determining if a relation is a function by drawing arrows from the domain values to the range values; in a function, each domain value will have only one range value

mean
a measure of central tendency that is the sum of the data values divided by the number of values; the average

median
a measure of central tendency that is the middle number in a set of data values

mode	a measure of central tendency that is the value that occurs most often in a set of data values
monomial	a polynomial of one term that consists of a number, a variable, or a product of numbers and/or variables

P

pattern	a set of numbers arranged in order
perfect square	a whole number whose square root is an integer
point-slope form	an equation of a line written in the form $(y - y_1) = m(x - x_1)$, where m is the slope and (x_1, y_1) is a point on the line
polynomial	an algebraic expression of one or more terms, in which the terms are joined by addition or subtraction
prime number	a natural number with exactly two factors, 1 and itself
properties of exponents	rules for operations with exponential expressions having the same base:

- to multiply, add the exponents: $x^a \cdot x^b = x^{(a + b)}$

- to divide, subtract the exponents: $\dfrac{x^a}{x^b} = x^{(a - b)}$

- to raise to a power, multiply the exponents: $(x^a)^b = x^{ab}$

Q

quartiles	three values that divide a set of data into four equal parts

- **first quartile** is the median of the lower half of the data
- **median,** or **second quartile,** divides the data into two equal parts
- **third quartile** is the median of the upper half of the data

R

range (of a relation)	the set of output, or y-, values for the dependent variables in a relation

range (of data)	a measure of dispersion or spread that is the difference between the greatest value and the least value in a set of data
rate of change	the amount a quantity changes over time; in a function, the slope of the line
rational expression	a fraction with polynomials for the numerator and denominator
rational number	a number that can be expressed as the ratio of two integers, $\frac{a}{b}$, where $b \neq 0$
real-number system	the set of all rational and irrational numbers
regression line	a line of best fit
relation	a set of ordered pairs or values

S

scatter plot	a graph that shows the relationship between two sets of data
slope	the measure of the steepness of a line, representing a rate of change; the ratio of vertical change (rise) to horizontal change (run)
slope formula	a formula for finding the slope (m) of a line, using any two points on the line (x_1, y_1) and (x_2, y_2) and $x_1 \neq x_2$ • $m = \frac{y_2 - y_1}{x_2 - x_1}$
slope-intercept form	an equation of a line written in the form $y = mx + b$, where m is the slope and b is the y-intercept
solution set	a set of points that satisfies an inequality
square	the product of a number multiplied by itself
square root	one of two equal factors of a number or expression
standard form	an equation of a line written in the form $ax + by = c$, where a, b, and c are constants and where a and b do not both equal zero

stem-and-leaf plot a graphic display that arranges data by place value and shows the shape of the data. The stem consists of the larger place values arranged in order; the leaves are the individual ones digits of every data value arranged in order adjacent to the relevant stem value.

substitution a method for solving systems of linear equations by rewriting one equation in terms of the other variable and then substituting the equivalent expression for that variable in the second equation

system of linear equations a set of two or more linear equations with the same variables that must be solved together

system of linear inequalities a set of two or more linear inequalities with the same variables that must be solved together

T

term part of an algebraic expression, consisting of a number, a variable, or the product of a number and variables

trinomial a polynomial of three terms

V

vertical-line test a test to determine if a relation is a function by drawing a vertical line through points; in a function, a vertical line passes through only one point at a time

X

x-intercept the x-coordinate of the point where the graph of an equation crosses the x-axis (when $y = 0$)

Y

y-intercept the y-coordinate of the point where the graph of an equation crosses the y-axis (when $x = 0$)

Glossary

Formula Sheet

You may use calculator π or the number 3.14.

Geometry

Rectangle:

$A = lw$

Rectangular Prism:

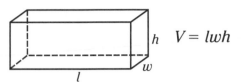

$V = lwh$

Arithmetic Properties

Additive Inverse:

$a + (\text{-}a) = 0$

Multiplicative Inverse:

$a \cdot \frac{1}{a} = 1$

Identity Property:

$a + 0 = a$

$a \cdot 1 = a$

Commutative Property:

$a + b = b + a$

$a \cdot b = b \cdot a$

Associative Property:

$(a + b) + c = a + (b + c)$

$(a \cdot b) \cdot c = a \cdot (b \cdot c)$

Distributive Property:

$a \cdot (b + c) = a \cdot b + a \cdot c$

Multiplicative Property of 0:

$a \cdot 0 = 0$

Additive Property of Equality:

If $a = b$, then $a + c = b + c$

Multiplicative Property of Equality:

If $a = b$, then $a \cdot c = b \cdot c$

Linear Equations

Slope:

$m = \frac{y_2 - y_1}{x_2 - x_1}$

Point-Slope Formula:

$(y - y_1) = m(x - x_1)$

Slope-Intercept Formula:

$y = mx + b$

Standard Equation of a Line:

$ax + by = c$